BUDDHISM

A Complete Guide to Discover the Secrets of Tibetan Buddhism

(Two Lectures on Buddhist Thought Concerning Esthetics)

Peter Potter

Published by Jackson Denver

Peter Potter

All Rights Reserved

Buddhism: A Complete Guide to Discover the Secrets of Tibetan Buddhism (Two Lectures on Buddhist Thought Concerning Esthetics)

ISBN 978-1-77485-162-3

All rights reserved. No part of this guide may be reproduced in any form without permission in writing from the publisher except in the case of brief quotations embodied in critical articles or reviews.

Legal & Disclaimer

The information contained in this book is not designed to replace or take the place of any form of medicine or professional medical advice. The information in this book has been provided for educational and entertainment purposes only.

The information contained in this book has been compiled from sources deemed reliable, and it is accurate to the best of the Author's knowledge; however, the Author cannot guarantee its accuracy and validity and cannot be held liable for any errors or omissions. Changes are periodically made to this book. You must consult your doctor or get professional medical advice before using any of the suggested remedies, techniques, or information in this book.

Upon using the information contained in this book, you agree to hold harmless the Author from and against any damages, costs, and expenses, including any legal fees potentially resulting from the application of any of the information provided by this guide. This disclaimer applies to any damages or injury caused by the use and application, whether directly or indirectly, of any advice or information presented, whether for breach of contract, tort, negligence, personal injury, criminal intent, or under any other cause of action.

You agree to accept all risks of using the information presented inside this book. You need to consult a professional medical practitioner in order to ensure you are both able and healthy enough to participate in this program.

TABLE OF CONTENTS

INTRODUCTION 1

CHAPTER 1: A FEW INFORMATION ABOUT BUDDHISM 4

CHAPTER 2: DAILY BUDDHISM PRACTICE 10

CHAPTER 3: FOUR NOBLE TRUTHS 30

CHAPTER 4: THE LIFE AND TEACHINGS OF BUDDHA 33

CHAPTER 5: THE TEACHINGS OF BUDDHA 48

CHAPTER 6: HOW BUDDHISM AND MEDITATION CAN ENLIGHTEN YOU 54

CHAPTER 7: THERAVADA, MAHAYANA, AND VAJRAYANA 60

CHAPTER 8: PHILOSOPHY CONTINUED: KARMA & DEATH & REBIRTH AND THE PROBLEMATIC EMOTIONS 66

CHAPTER 9: BUDDHIST WORSHIP 74

CHAPTER 10: REINCARNATION: WHY IS IT IMPORTANT IN BUDDHISM? 78

CHAPTER 11: BUILDING MINDFUL AND MEANINGFUL RELATIONSHIPS 106

CHAPTER 12: LET'S PRACTICE! 109

CHAPTER 13: BUDDHIST TRADITIONS 140

CHAPTER 14: PRECEPT AND RIGHT ACTION 149

CHAPTER 15: THE DO'S AND DON'TS OF BUDDHISM 159

CHAPTER 16: WHAT IS SUFFERING?.............................. 166

CHAPTER 17: RESPECTING YOUR POSTURE................... 173

CHAPTER 18: BUDDHA'S PHILOSOPHY - HOW DOES IT INTEGRATE INTO YOUR DAILY LIFE? 178

CONCLUSION... 189

Introduction

What are you most passionate about? What would you choose if you could have everything you want? This question could be asked to fifty people and you would get fifty different responses. However, regardless of their answers, there would be one common desire: to be happy. We want happiness, love, relationships, money and a better life. A Buddhist parable says something similar:

One poor man wanders the country, beggaring for food and coins from strangers. The friend is a friend that the poor man hasn't seen in many years. He felt sorry for him and invited him to his house to have a decent meal, and to have a comfortable bed to sleep in. The friend, unlike the poor man was wealthy and led a luxurious lifestyle.

The friend sneaked in to the room where the poor man was asleep and sewn a precious jewel into the lining of his robe. The poor man thanked his friend and continued his wanderings through the countryside the next day.

The years passed before the friend and the poor man met again. The friend saw that the poor man was still living his life by begging and struggling. He was unaware of the precious jewel hidden in his robe. He was a poor man who had enough money to buy everything he wanted but he lived a life of poverty and insecurity.

In that most of us desire happiness, we are like the poor man. Our lives are a constant pursuit of the things, people, and situations that will make us happy. We are unable to see the infinite source of happiness within ourselves because our attention is fixed on external things. As the poor man couldn't see the treasure in his robes, so too can we fail to recognize that every person has the precious jewel of insight.

Our lives will never be free from endless cycles of our desires and attempts at satisfying them, unless we realize this. This is our life's backdrop, and we play a part in the cosmic play. It is okay to have desires and work towards achieving them. It is both necessary and enjoyable to have these desires. Problem arises when our life circumstances influence our self-worth and identity. This can lead to a feeling of lack and limitation in your life. Realize this gem within you and you will find true happiness.

This is the purpose and goal of Buddhism: to find this precious jewel. This is a special journey that will lead to profound discoveries.

Chapter 1: A Few Information about

Buddhism

Since many years, the spiritual school of Buddhism has existed. It all began in northern India with Siddhartha Gatama, a young nobleman who realized that not all the riches of the world made him happy. He quit his luxurious lifestyle to explore the world in search of true happiness. He tried many different ways to make himself and others happy.

Legend has it that the Buddha fell into deep meditation for 49 days after he reached the Bodgi tree at the age of 35. He had already reached Enlightenment, and understood the path humans must follow to achieve their own nirvana. This idea would end their reincarnation cycles, and help them to stop the suffering and pain caused by karma.

The Buddha wasn't sure at first if he should share his findings with others. He was worried they wouldn't believe him and that they would be too selfish or mean to want to know more about his teachings. The Buddha came around, however, and shared his knowledge about the Four Noble Truths, and the Eightfold Path. He explained how your actions today will create karma. This will force you to reincarnate in order to correct the karma you created.

Buddhism has many teachings and is a spiritual school that has survived the test of time. We will only discuss a few aspects of this to keep it simple.

The Four Noble Truths are the first. These truths are essential for every Buddhist to believe. These truths basically say that there is suffering and that people will have dissatisfaction and cravings in this world. They get jealous of others and want more of the things they don't have. This will lead to karma that causes them pain and comes back. These problems can be solved by following the Eightfold Path's good deeds, and actions.

Buddhists learn the basics of how to act if they want to achieve their nirvana, ending the cycle of karma or reincarnation with the Eightfold Path. These can be very detailed, but they are essentially about how to act as a good person and how to choose occupations that don't cause harm to animals or people, how to speak, think and act with kindness and much more.

These tenets will reverse your karma and prevent you from experiencing another incarnation. Buddhists believe that this life's pain and suffering is directly related to your past karma. You may regret your past actions to animals or other people. You can overcome the evil in the lives most people lead and begin to get rid of the pain and suffering.

A fascinating idea from Buddhism is that you might not always return as a human during reincarnation. You may be reincarnated as animals, plants, or a combination of both. Many Buddhists have a strong connection with animals and the natural world. These Buddhists know they have to treat animals with respect, especially if the animal is going to return in the next life.

The ultimate goal for a Buddhist is to attain nirvana. To reach nirvana, they must follow the Eightfold path. This includes meditation and self-reflection. You can end the cycle of reincarnation by completing the Eightfold path, which includes meditation and self-reflection. You can now live in peace and happiness after you have reached this place.

Some people find Buddhism a bit too mystical for their liking. Some people may feel that the concept of karma or enlightenment is too complicated for them. Others may feel this religion is too old or too mysterious to be incorporated into their daily lives.

This religion has also stood the test of times. This religion has been followed by people for hundreds of centuries. You can see its followers all over the world. Many people feel the tenets of Buddhism speak to them and can help them live a better life. Although you might not believe all that Buddhism has to offer, there are so many benefits that this religion is still relevant for modern life.

This religion asks you to let go of the impermanent things that cause you unhappiness and make your modern life difficult. You can make a huge difference in your quality of life by learning how to let go and stop causing damage to yourself and others.

These tenets are still important to many people today. These ideas are still valuable and can be used to help you achieve the happiness you desire.

Although some of these ideas are rooted in an ancient religion, many can still be applied to your everyday life. Many of the principles you'll find in Buddhism are about being a good person, and being kind to other people. This is something we can all relate to and strive for, even if Buddhism is not the right religion. This guidebook will explain how the different tenets work, and why they are important for helping you live a happy life regardless of your religion.

Chapter 2: Daily Buddhism Practice

The Buddha Dharma does not consist of a collection of words. It is clearly a product of experience. Some people think Buddhism and Buddha Dharma are a collection or knowledge. However, if this knowledge remains too low, it is not enough. Dualistic thinking is a state in which the Buddha's teachings must be applied at all times. Until we realize Emptiness, our dualistic mind will continue to function. This means that we must apply the Buddha Dharma every moment of our lives.

Some people think that the Buddha Dharma can only be learned from books or teachers. However, once we leave the group, it is no longer something that is present in our minds. While group discussions and practice are important, it's equally important to keep Buddha Dharma alive in all aspects of your daily life.

It is possible to think that many things in life have nothing to do with the dharma. However, this is a false concept. The dharma can be applied at any moment in our lives. You may find it funny or bizarre to think that this moment has nothing to do dharma. But if you take the time to analyze it, you'll see that there is a level at which the dharma can apply. Dharma, or the power or ability of transforming any situation into something spiritual, depends on your motivation. Motivation is the key word. It is important to meditate as often as possible about our motivation. What is our goal What is our goal in life? What are we hoping to accomplish in this life? Our right motivation must be to help others, since we are part of the Mahayana tradition. All of our thinking and actions must be directed toward the benefit others. This could be our deepest desire, thought, or goal: To benefit others. This does not mean we should neglect our lives, our interests or our bodies. It just means we need to be mindful of our health and how it affects our body. With that motivation, any moment can be made wonderful.

Today, I took the shower as an example. This seems to be an everyday occurrence. We may not even think about what we're doing while we take a shower. We may be thinking about many other things while cleaning our bodies. If we look at the act of cleaning our bodies, and transform it in the right manner, it can be transformed into a Purification practice. While soap cleans our bodies, we can also generate the desire to cleanse our minds from their delusions. This thought can completely transform the situation. Although it sounds funny, this is actually a powerful tool that helps to purify our minds.

This can be used to transform almost all of your activities. You can transform a garden that has weeds into a place where you can pull out the roots of cyclic existence.

You may feel like you are cleansing your mind of the three poisons while you sweep the apartment's floor.

The meal is an excellent moment to practice. This is a great way to meditate simultaneously on attachment and Bodhicitta. There are many conceptions that can arise when you look at what's on your plate. These could be attachment or aversion to the food. This is the time to reflect and meditate on these concepts. You must also ask yourself why you eat, and why your body is in good health. Good health is important, even if you eat healthy food. But the motivation to eat the meal must be to improve your mind and reach the ultimate goal of helping more sentient beings. This motivation means that we don't eat more to satisfy our hunger, but eat to help others.

Every moment that you can see as an opportunity to transform can be a dharma-practice. It is important to keep our attention on this, as most of our time is not spent in an "official practice", [reciting] sadhana, etc., but in everyday activities.

People think that they live a miserable life because they can't retire to a cave and practice as many solitary meditations or retreats as they want, but it is just as effective to practice daily. Sure, being able to retire can give you a deeper engagement with the dharma. However, it is possible to stay in the current life and transform it into a dharma-practice if you have the right motivation.

First, it is important that you keep the Six Perfections in mind. This will allow us to focus more on one of these perfections in many aspects of our day. It is important to meditate every morning before we open our eyes. This will give our day the right direction, the right impulse, and help us make the right decision to do our best to follow the dharma teachings. It is crucial because it will help us to have a higher level of awareness.

Two qualities are essential to keep in mind in practice and daily life. They are awareness and memory. Awareness is a quality that warns us when our mind develops a negative aspect. When we recognize that our mind is not moving in the right direction, we can remember the correct direction. We can change our mindset to be more positive.

Instead of viewing difficult situations as negative or stressful, we should seek the best solution according to the dharma every time we face them. Instead of seeing a large portion of our lives as a burden, we should see it as an opportunity to practice. As we progress on the dharma path, we are more likely to engage in advanced paths like the Tantric path. This will help us transform our daily lives into practice.

In addition to the motivation, there is a practice called Shinein Tibetan that can be used regularly. It is a mental calmness that is important. Our mind is often not focused, which can lead to many problems, including the causes and manifestations of mental disorders. The mind is often not calm at all and jumps from one idea to the next, from fear to another or from one wish to another.

The real way to practice dharma is in the way we deal with our minds and with what we refer to as 'outside circumstances'. Each word has its own significance, and each technical point [of dharma] has its own importance. But even if your knowledge is extensive and you have memorized many texts, you won't be able to apply the dharma every time you think about it. We have all the information, all the texts, there is a lot more data support, computers, and cds. It is no longer necessary to memorize a huge amount of texts. However, it is important to be able to handle the current situations. While living in Sera monastery, there were many monks. Some were high scholars, others were simple monks. However, it wasn't always the high scholars that are the most successful. While I don't have anything against scholastic learning, the scholastic information becomes meaningful when it is applied to daily life. There is a propensity in the west to place a lot emphasis on diploma and other scholastic degrees. Many high lamas don't have a degree but are amazing at explaining the dharma. When I think about this, I think about Lama Yeshe and Kyabje Zpa Rinpoche, who, while they may not have a Geshe degree as such, their ability to explain the Dharma is amazing. It is practical, it is applicable.

Each of you are making progress on the dharma pathway and each one of you wants to engage more. I believe it is important to keep your focus on the practice, to learn how to apply it, to change your mind. This is more important than memorizing texts or spending months learning Tibetan. It is okay to have enough energy and time to learn Tibetan. This should not be the main focus. It is important to focus on how we interact with our children, spouse, boss, and other people. This is crucial because in all these situations, we create the karmas that will shape our future. Talking about children, it's how we deal with them and how they are taught the dharma principles. This will help them get those good principles in an effective way.

As soon as we become known as a Buddhist practitioner, it is also a responsibility to others by the way we behave in daily life. This is not about pretending to being something we aren't, but trying to be the best version of ourselves. As we engage in the path, I expect -- at least, I do -- to get better and better each time I have the chance to practice. All the formal rituals and practices are there to assist you in this way. The core of the dharma lifestyle, the core practice is our motivation and how we apply it every day.

I was referring to shine as an important practice. Once we have a good understanding of shine, it's important to use our quiet mind to a topic such as emptiness. It is important to be able to see the world as it is, and not just grasp the details. The basis of Buddhism is not in complex sadhanas or complicated practices. It lies in the way we deal with common phenomena. Again, I don't have anything against rituals or studies. But I believe we need to be more flexible. Although it might seem odd, many people still rely on ritual and scholastic study more than others, many holy beings have found that our mental state is the most helpful.

Recent events in America have brought us into contact with many questions. People may ask us what we think, how do we analyze it, and other such questions. It is in these moments that dharma must 'show itself'. It is important that we have a stable mind and a strong Bodhicitta motivation when considering what might happen in the future.

Bodhicitta goes beyond Compassion, as it is often translated into the west. Bodhicitta can be better described as Awakening Mind. It refers to a mental state that thinks altruistically about all sentient beings. While we think in an altruistic manner about all sentient creatures, there is a deep desire to participate in the relief of all the suffering. This is an engagement that transcends time and space, with no boundaries. This is important because we can make class distinctions between human beings based on different circumstances. It is easy to make categories among humans, which can lead to a form of xenophobia or a form of racism towards another group. It is important to recognize the difference between the behaviours of people and the being, or consciousness itself. While we may disagree with certain behaviors, it is possible to show disagreements but not make judgments about the being. You can disagree with fascism if you're in the presence of one, but you cannot take away from someone your compassion. When confronted with a particular ideology for whatever reason, it is important to try to find an antidote without being hateful towards those who are behind.

This principle can also be applied to everyday life. While we might not agree with every aspect of an attack by the talibans, we should never hate any aspect.

If you find yourself in a situation where someone is angry, displaying hatred, or any other wrong ideology, then you can try to take a position before the ideology, without having to fight against a person. This could be used in many situations where the appearance and the being are mixed. When we aren't happy with what they are showing or what they are expressing, we tend to be hostile towards beings.

We must remember that violence is not a solution to violence. This is especially true when we are confronted with the things we don't appreciate. Gandhi said, "Eye by Eye, the World will Be Blind Soon." It is important to reflect on these things because we are in degenerating times and many events are proving that we are not getting the best. As dharma practitioners, we must be clear on how to respond to different situations.

Q. Q. Could you please explain some similarities between the Islamic concept Djihad and Buddhist Shambala warrior? I sometimes think about the fact these people believe they are very good and are serving their god. But they do very bad things.

A. A. Shambala warriors never go against beings. They never oppose the reality of a being, his consciousness. For those who are familiar with Shambala, it's a way to fight negative influences. We could see some wrathful Buddhists, for instance. So, there's a fight against negativities but not against beings. What we call 'warriors' or 'heros to liberation' or whatever they are, is really a struggle for the best for all beings and for the promotion of freedom for all beings. Djihad is motivated to promote one side only, their side. I find this concept to be unbearable. They believe that the more people who don't follow their religion, the higher their rank in heaven. The object is different. We could learn a lot from this. We can learn a lot from those who are trying to achieve a goal. What are our willingness to do daily dharma practice? What are you willing to do for others? If those people are willing to die to achieve their goals, how can we think of engaging our entire life in the service of others? This is what we can ask when we meditate about our motivations, about Bodhicitta.

Q. It is difficult for me to distinguish the actions of beings and their beings.

A. A. There are many layers to that consciousness, including misconceptions, social educations and misunderstandings. This causes the consciousness to react inappropriately most of the times. The texts say that the consciousness is all-knowing and clear. Each consciousness is capable of this clarity. However, due to the many karmic causes we have created and all the misconceptions we have, we are not able to access it. We do react to our egos, and all the other misconceptions. This is what we need to see when someone reacts. You don't need to look at others. We can also look at our reactions when we are angry. For example, you can meditate on this: What made me angry? Are you angry because of your true fundamental Buddha nature? Is it my true fundamental Buddha nature that got angry? You know the answer. We can then ask ourselves the same question when someone else gets angry. This is because they have misunderstood or misunderstood us, and we can find a way of reacting to this misunderstanding but not against the person who is behind. So I could say, "I don't like anger", but not: "I don't like this being". This allows us to work on our own misconceptions and avoid the anger at others.

Q. Q.

A. In such cases, we must separate the action, how we react, and the motivation to do so. We will not engage in harmful activities if we have the right motivation. However, we won't have to fight to help others. It is clear that when someone tries to attack your children, I mean "to fight".

This implies that we must do all that is necessary to protect their well-being. However, we must do it with the right motivation. How we are emotionally engaging in the relationship with the attacker and children is the key to finding the right motivation. We could summarize it as "the limit" of our activities being the death [not the life]. You may be a skilled fighter and try to save your children's lives by fighting. But the limit must be the life of the attacker. It is not possible to act for the benefit of killing. There is no justification for killing.

This is a complex subject because it involves both our emotions as well as a lot of attachments. Since we often don't have the right view of cause and condition, it can be difficult to figure out the best way to deal with such situations. It is better to prepare yourself by meditation on emotions, motivation, and interdependence of phenomena so that you can face any situation later.

Q. Q.

A. Everything is driven by motivation. You might be familiar with the Bodhisattva story, who had to kill someone to save a boat. This story is interesting. We can all agree that killing is a negative action. However, the story of the bodhisattva who killed one person and was willing to kill 500 others is a good example.

Q. Q.

A. A. He didn't kill that person to save 500 others. To avoid 500 more murders, he wanted to kill the person. This is slightly different because it is impossible to avoid the fact that the causes they have caused are being met. No matter what we do, if someone has caused the karma for death, they will be killed. However, if someone wants to kill, it is not karmically constrained. It is your free will to do so. You can therefore act on it. Many people believe that the bodhisattva killed the person to save 500 lives. However, this is false. To avoid the possibility of that person committing 500 murders, he killed that person. We can safely say that he has attained the negative karma of killing a man because he killed one man. However, his motive was pure and the act was done for the benefit of the other man, so the negative aspects are covered.

If we want to stop something from happening, we need to quickly analyze why we are doing it and find the right motivation. If you need to punch someone to save another person, there is no negative in it. The motivation is right. Even though it might seem negative just for the fact that you have to punch someone, the negativity would be covered by the right motivation - if the motivation was right.

Bodhicitta was the motivation behind the Bodhisattva's killing of a person. He had Bodhicitta. Not just the idea or taste of Bodhicitta but the actualization of Bodhicitta. It is not the act that is important. It is the motivation behind the action. If you do have to fight one day, I wouldn't say it creates negative karma if you are fighting for something that is motivated by Bodhicitta. I would add that the bodhisattva vows clearly state that we must not avoid acting in a wrathful manner if it is in the best interest of sentient beings. The bodhisattva ideal of 'I am not violent and I cannot do any violence' is too clear. It seems violent. Violence is not in the movement; it is in the motivation. Some people appear calm but can be very violent in their words and their behavior. Others are rude and rough, but they have a great motivation. You understand?

You can think about the wrathful gods. Mahakala, for instance, is Chenrezig's emanation and is the embodiment compassion. Mahakala on the other hand is terrifying, with his head cut off, and so forth. However, the wrathful element does not necessarily mean angry motivation. It is important to distinguish between what we see and what lies behind.

Q. Q. Do you believe that there will be a third world war?

A. We can summarize by saying that we must pray for world peace because it will happen what the largest number of people [karmically] created. It doesn't matter if there is a third world conflict or not. However, the future seems less peaceful. Without any emotion, we must pray as much as possible. Two things are required of us: first, we must pray to be able and willing to help in any situation. Second, we must pray to see peace. It is not necessary to be optimistic or pessimistic if we know the law of cause-and-effect. Instead, it is better to just wait to see what happens outside and to spiritually grow inside. Although we cannot alter the outcome of the large number of beings that have created it, we can make changes inside and therefore can have an impact on what happens outside.

Chapter 3: Four Noble Truths

The Four Noble Truths are the one aspect of Buddhism that best describes the entire religion. These truths were first revealed by Buddha in his first sermon and have since been the foundation of Buddhism as it is today. These truths are:

The truth about suffering (dukkha).

Dukkha is anything that is conditional. It is anything that can pass or is not permanent. It is possible to translate the first Noble Truth as "life is suffering." This might seem strange, especially for those who are just starting Buddhism. Buddha explained the truth of this truth. It is about understanding that we are not immortal and neither are our feelings or suffering. Dukkha is everything that begins and ends. This includes happiness, sadness, grief, and all other matters. Buddha taught that it was important to understand our'self' before considering the concepts of death and life.

Samudaya: The truth about the cause of suffering

The second truth is that we suffer because we want what we don't have. This universal truth is undisputed: our desires are endless. We want more as soon as we have it. We tend to envy the plates of others and look at them. We want to have what others have and we neglect what we have. This is called jealousy and it's worse than any other emotion.

Buddha said that pursuing worldly goods can lead to our losing ourselves and our path. We get so attached to material possessions, opinions, ideas and the like that we become upset when things don't go our way. This, Buddha emphasizes, is what causes suffering.

This is a simple lesson that all of us can relate to. We often wonder why we don't have the same opportunities to see others who have more. We aren't content to look at those who have less and be thankful, but we always want more. This preoccupation can be eliminated and we can find true happiness.

The truth about the end of suffering (nirhodha).

After explaining what suffering is, Buddha taught how to heal it. He said that practice was the key to the cure. We can achieve the stage of enlightenment by becoming stronger and not giving into our ever-expanding desires.

It is important to keep trying, to look the other way, and to control our urges when confronted with overwhelming feelings. This may be the most difficult thing we have ever to do but it is the path to true liberation.

The truth about the path that relieves us of suffering (magga).

Buddha stressed the importance of believing, and he taught that it was not enough. It's not enough to just know and talk. It is important to practice it. You can refer to the Eightfold Path as the path he taught.

Chapter 4: The Life and Teachings of

Buddha

Siddhartha Gautama's life is full of lessons. We have already spoken of his royal birth and how he tried to understand the world in a deeper way. He explored existential topics such as happiness, pain and death. He tried to understand reality. He spent time understanding the heart of each person and then created his teachings to bring about happiness.

Buddha's teachings are based upon the idea of happiness and peace. These ideas are not abstract concepts but important steps in our daily lives. A person can thrive in any situation by understanding who they are and the realities of life. Siddhartha was born to the royal family of Kapilavastu. He decided that his life in the palace was too extravagant and that he would make many trips to explore the world outside of the palace walls. Buddha found four things that made his life better: death, sickness, and a monk who gave up everything he had to end suffering. Siddhartha made the decision to follow in the footsteps of the monk after his fourth trip. To symbolize his renunciation of the worldly lifestyle, he cut his hair and left his kingdom. He then began to wander as a monk, and called himself Gautama. He traveled from one place to the next, in ragged robes, searching for truth. Although he practiced asceticism, he faced many hardships. But, just like his life as a royal, it didn't take him anywhere. He realized that too much hardship wouldn't bring him happiness, and started eating healthy and nutritious food again. While sitting under the Bodhi tree, he experienced enlightenment and deep meditation. Mara, the evil one, tried to tempt him but Gautama defeated Mara by his virtue. Buddha, instead of being seduced by Mara (the evil one), discovered what causes suffering and how to end it.

The three universal truths Buddha discovered during his enlightenment were the following:

* Everything is not lost in the universe. According to Buddha, there is no loss in the world. This is due to the fact that matter turns into energy and energy into matter. Like plants, people are made from the things around them. You are only destroying yourself when you destroy the world around you. You are only hurting your self if you inflict pain on another person. This will teach you to be kind to your environment and others. You should first consider the good of others when you seek good for yourself.

* Everything changes - This second universal truth confirms that all things in life are constantly changing. Buddha said that life is like a flowing river. Life can be both tranquil and chaotic, just as a river flows at times. Sometimes the river may encounter rocks, and it does not flow smoothly. These rocky moments are part of life and can be accepted as part of the process. This universal truth teaches us that the things we have been taught can change. This forces us to change our outlook and approach to life.

* Law of cause-and-effect - Many refer to this as karma. It says that nothing happens by chance and that people attract what they want. Your actions, words and emotions are the most important factors in what you get, no matter how good or bad. Simply put, if you do good things, good things will follow. If you do bad, bad things will follow. According to Buddha, we create karma through what we think, say and do. Karma is a friend and a change in your life. Understanding karma will help you see the path to a brighter future.

The Four Noble Truths: Teachings

After his enlightenment, the sermon of Buddha was said to have been focused on the four noble truths. These truths are the foundation of Buddhism as they provide guidelines and help people achieve spiritual awakening. These are described below.

There is Suffering (Dukkha).

Dukkha could also be translated as "life is suffering". Buddha said that all of life is a struggle or suffering. This means that there's no way to find happiness or fulfillment in our lives. You should not allow circumstances and experiences to determine your happiness. Many of the things people attach happiness or feelings to are temporary, conditional or made up of other things. Dukkha is the term for material possessions you consider valuable and fun. They will eventually end. Instead, be you and embrace every moment instead of clinging on to past achievements or events. Your own self-created happiness is the most valuable thing.

You must also accept that suffering is real and not live in fear. Accepting it is part of you and will not allow it to destroy your inner self. We will all experience four things: death, sickness, old-age, and birth. This means that all these sufferings are inevitable. Because we all experience pain, suffering, and happiness, your happiness will not last forever. This knowledge will allow you to live in the present, not regret your past, and stop worrying about what the future holds.

Every Suffering Has a Cause

A second truth is that your suffering is never unavoidable. He said that many people suffer from ignorance of the law of Karma and greed for wrong pleasures. Our minds and bodies are hurt by the steps we take to find happiness and enjoy life. All of us need adequate shelter, food and clothing. However, we must also enjoy and value life, regardless how basic. You can probably imagine a situation in which an individual receives money, such as a large inheritance. While they will enjoy the benefits and want more, it is greed that causes feelings of inadequacy and disappointment. Understanding the root cause of your suffering can help you avoid it completely, leading to a happier and more fulfilling life. This truth shows us that our desire for external things is the root cause of our suffering. When in fact, the power to make us happy lies within us. They will never be happy, no matter how successful they are. Satisfaction is the key to true success. It's what makes you happy and gives you peace.

Every Suffering Has an End

This truth gives us hope, the Buddha. The Buddha gives us hope by revealing the root cause of the problem (Dukkha). It is your responsibility to not be greedy or ignorant if you want to end your suffering. It's about changing your outlook and living a peaceful life. You can be certain that all the suffering and pain will go away when you do this. According to Buddhist teachings, Nirvana is the point at which your suffering ceases. This is one of the most positive messages in Buddhism. It is the realization that even though suffering is real, there is a way to get out. The mind and the state of a person are key factors in suffering. You can eliminate suffering by changing your thoughts and mind.

The Path to Ending Suffering

The fourth noble truth is the path to ending suffering. This is more than just about ending your own suffering. You will help others by taking control of your mind, body and emotions. The fourth noble truth is the foundation of the eightfold path.

*   Right view - This is the ability to see and understand things as they really are and recognize the importance of the four noble truths.

* Right intention - This describes the mental energy that controls our actions and gives us the ability to improve ourselves. There are three types right intentions. The first is the intention to renounce or resist desire. Intention of goodwill - resisting anger feelings. Intention of innocence - not acting or thinking violently, cruelly or aggressively.

* Right speech - Your words have the power to affect others in many different ways. They can save or destroy lives, make friends, or create a lasting peace, or even start a terrible conflict. Avoid false speech, slanderous speech and idle chatter. You will be able to communicate well with others, tell the truth and build friendships.

* Right action - This refers to actions that involve your bodily functions. It's about avoiding harming others, stealing, or sexual misconduct. You can be kind to other people, be honest, respect their belongings, and have sexual relationships with them if you take the right steps.

* Right livelihood - This emphasises the importance to earn your living legally. The Buddha says that slavery, dealing with weapons, meat production, and selling poisons and intoxicants are all things that can harm others and should be avoided.

* Right effort - This shows that you can't achieve anything without hard work.

* Right mindfulness - This describes an individual's ability see things exactly as they are and have a clear mind.

* Right concentration - Focus on positive thoughts and actions. This is a method of improving your meditation skills in order to attain enlightenment.

Chapter 5: The Teachings Of Buddha

This chapter and the next will present the fundamental dostrinedz for earlu Buddhism. They were adz displayed modztlu in the Pali Canon. Theu've been the guiding framework of all new develormentdz since the Theravada.

Buddhidzm begins and ends in a feeling. This idz the greatestedzt origin Buddhidzt teachings and sertainlu is direct towardsdz religious and etheal development culminating in an adventure of like sharaster. The Buddha was able to immediately learn about rebirth, karma, and the four "True Realities for Spiritually Ennobled". One or more of the three basic teashingdz in early Buddhism could be organized by one of these heads.

Idz Buddhidzm an Ethical Sudztem?

Buddhism has an extraordinary moral code, one for monkdz, and another for laity. However, it is more than an ordinaru moral teashing.

It is only the first dztage of the Path of Puritu. It is the first dztage of the Path of Puritu.

The foundation of Buddhidzm is made up of the Four Noble Truthdz. The firdzt three rerredzent rhilodzorhu teachings of Buddha; the fourth ethisdz of Buddhidzm based on that philosophy.

Buddhidzm's morality is not based on a doubtful divine revelation nor the ingenious inventions of an exceptional mind. It is a rational and rrastisal way of thinking that is based on verifiable facts.

Professor Rhudz Daviddz states: "Buddhidzt, or no Buddhist, I have examined all the great religioudz dzudztemdz; in none of thodze has I found anything to dzurradzdz i beautu and somrrehendzivenedzdz The Noble Eightfold Path to the Buddha.

It is important to remember that according to Buddhidzm, there are deeds which are good and bad and deeddz that are neither good or bad. However, when one reaches the ultimate goal of the Holy Life, one can transdzsendz both good and harm.

The Buddha dzaudz:"Righteous thingdz(dhamma)uou have to give ur:how mush more the unrighteoudz things (adhamma)." The deed whish idz adzdzosiated with attashment(lobha), ill-will(dodza)and delusion(moha)idz evil.That deed whish is adzdzosiated with non-attashment(alobha), goodwill(adodza), and widzdom(ranna), idz good.

An Arahant is a Stainledzdz one. His deedz have no ethisal value.

Hidz actions, in Pali, are called kiriya(funstional).Puredzt gold sannot further be rurified.

The mental dztatedz of the four types of supramundane Path sondzsioudznedzdz, namelu, Sotapatti(Stream-Winner), Sakadagami(Onse-Returner), Anagami(Non-Returner)and Arahatta(Worthu), though wholesome(kudzala), do not tend to assumulate fresh Kamma, but, on the sontraru, tend to the gradual cessation of the individual flux of besoming, and therewith to the gradual sedzdzation of good and evil deeddz.In thedze types of dzurramundane sondzsioudznedzdz the wisdom fastor(ranna), whish tenddz to destroy the rootdz of Kamma, idz rredominant; while inthe mundane turedz of consciousness volition(setana)whish produces Kammis activities is predominant.

What is the sriterion for morality assording Buddhism?

The Buddha's admonition to uoung Samanera Rakula provides the answer.

Rahula says that if there is a deed to be done, Rahula should say: Is this deed harmful to me, others, or both? This is a terrible deed that causes suffering.

"If you have a deed that you want to do, think about this: Is it not harmful to me, to others, or to both? You mudzt repeat a bad deed that causes harm to others.

Buddhidzt, in adzdzedzdzing moralitu, takes into consideration the interedztdz of himdzelf as well as other animals - animaldz not exempt.

The Karaniua Metta Sutta is where the Buddha exhortsz:

"Adz the mother rrotestdz she only shild even at her ridzk; even dzo let us cultivate boundledzdz thoughtdz toward all being."

The Dhammarada Dztatedz

"All fear runidzhment to all life idz precious.

One must read the Dhammarada and Sigalovada Sutas, Vuaggharajja Sutas, Mangala Sutas, Metta Sutas, Parabhava Sutas, Vadzala Sutas, Dhammika Sutas to understand the exertionallu high standards of moralitu that Buddha exrestdzz from His ideal followers.

Adz a moral teashing, it exseldz every other ethisal dzudztemdz. But moralitu idz only onlu at the beginning and not at the end of Buddhidzm.

One dzendze Buddhism is not a "rhilodzorhu", while another dzendze Buddhism is the philosophy of "rhilodzorhiedz".

Chapter 6: How Buddhism and Meditation Can Enlighten You

The concepts of "awakening" or "enlightenment" are related to the concept "no self". This is what sets Buddhism apart from all other religions and philosophical systems. Actually, "Buddha" means "The Awakened One", which is why Buddhism's core is made up of this awakening.

People often adopt Buddhism and start to practice it because of the promise of enlightenment. The Eightfold Path is the path to liberation and enlightenment. We will explain the Eightfold Path concept in detail:

The Right View: This is understanding the "right" way to perceive the world. It allows one to see the internal and outer aspects of human life with no preconceived notions or prejudices. These things can be understood simply as they are without judgment or preconceived notions.

The Right Discipline: One must stop trying to complicate things in order to attain enlightenment. You can achieve this by not setting unrealistic expectations about how things should look and learning to accept the world as it is.

The Right Intention: What is behind a person's actions or words? Poor intentions are often caused by insecurity about the future, a desire for financial gains or jealousy. Buddhism encourages people to be grateful for what they have and to do everything with the best intentions. Every action should not cause harm to anyone.

The Right Speech: A speech that is true and honest comes from the heart. If one works purely with their brain, without any heart, their thoughts, words and actions will be manipulative and have harmful intentions. Buddhism suggests that one should speak only from the heart when speaking. These are the real feelings, which are free of manipulation or harm.

The Right Approach: If one puts in the effort, one can change their outlook from one that is outcome-oriented to one that focuses on process. They will be able to see situations as they are and accept them. This could be a paradigm shift that can change your life.

The Right Life: Buddhism encourages people to do their best with the resources they have. It is said that "bloom where your planted," means that you should do the best with what you have. They should not feel that their talents can be better used elsewhere. Instead, they should give their full attention to the task at hand. They shouldn't waste their time wishing they could be somewhere else. They can work hard to make the necessary changes in their lives outside of work.

The Right Concentration: Our minds can wander and we often operate in "autopilot mode". Meditation helps us discipline our minds to stay in the present moment and not in the future or past.

The Right Mindfulness: Being mindful is the ability to notice the smallest details of your personality, your habits, your traits, and the events in your life. This includes body language, verbal communication, work effort, thoughts, feelings and emotions. This awareness will give you a greater understanding of your life, actions and thoughts and allow you to feel more confident about where you stand on certain issues.

The goal of meditation in Buddhism is to attain enlightenment. This can be achieved by learning and mastering The Eightfold Path concepts. These qualities are key to achieving nirvana. Nirvana refers to a state of bliss in which all suffering is ended and all negativity is eliminated.

These are some tips to help you reach enlightenment or nirvana within your life.

Keep your eyes on the present. Reality exists only in the moment. Everything else is a movie your mind creates or replays with the help perception and emotion.

Concentrate more. Your mind is like a butterfly, it likes to move from one topic to the next. It is very difficult to stay focused and fully focus on one thing without being distracted. But, if you are able cultivate this ability and attain it, you can control your life!

Non-attachment is a practice that you can do. Attachment is the desire for more and can lead to a disconnect between your actions, and your true self. This doesn't mean you have to stop loving other people. This means that you should feel the love and affection of someone without attachment.

Regular meditation is a good idea. Meditation can help you focus better and remove yourself from the distractions of daily life. This will allow you to take control of your thoughts. Spend at least 15 minutes a day in silence, meditating. This will make positive changes in your life and allow you to follow the Eightfold Path to Enlightenment.

A person's perceptions and visions of the world are limited before they can attain enlightenment. They are not able to see the full potential and nature of their lives. After attaining enlightenment, a person can see themselves and the world in the same way as someone who was blind before they gained sight.

Buddhism teaches that peace in the mind is essential for true peace. The above concepts can help you achieve peace of mind. These concepts will become more real in your life with practice. This will allow you to be less afraid and ensure that all your thoughts and actions are for the good of those around you.

Chapter 7: Theravada, Mahayana, And Vajrayana

This chapter, and the following, will describe the different orders or schools of Buddhism. This will enable you to compare the differences and similarities among Buddhist practitioners from different parts of the globe. This chapter covers the three oldest Buddhist traditions--Theravada, Mahayana, and Vajrayana.

All three forms of Vajrayana Buddhism, Mahayana and Theravada are practiced around the world. However, most people are drawn to Asia.

Theravada

Theravada is the oldest school in Buddhism. Theravada followers consider their tradition to the best preserved of the earliest schools and traditions of Buddhism. They believe only the Buddha's earliest collected teachings are true dharma.

These early teachings are known as the Pali Canon. Pali is a language spoken in Gautama Buddha's time. Although the Pali Canon is the only authentic dharma in Buddhism's traditions, some schools also accept other collected teachings.

The Theravadan tradition states that monks who live in monasteries play a different role than the average layperson. Theravada Buddhism is a common religion. Societies that are open to laypeople provide support for monks who seek spiritual enlightenment. The majority of Theravada is practiced in Southeast Asian countries.

Mahayana

Mahayana Buddhism is more common in the Northern and Far Eastern parts of Asia. They also consider the Pali Canon sacred text like Theravadan Buddhists. However, Mahayana Buddhists hold later Sanskrit sutras to be sacred texts. The Mahayana tradition doesn't distinguish between monks or laypeople. Spiritual awakening practices are more accessible to everyone.

Mahayana is closely related to Zen Buddhism, and this relationship will be explored more under Western Buddhism.

Mahayana Buddhists are more likely to practice rituals and ceremonies that Theravadan Buddhists. They are also more likely to use icons, figures, and other imagery. The Theravadan tradition claims that it is the closest descendant of Gautama Buddha's original teachings, but Mahayana Buddhists insist that they are a more accurate representation of Buddha's teachings. These two schools of Buddhism don't work in opposition to each other.

Many regional schools of Buddhism in China and Japan are also influenced by Mahayana teachings. Zen Buddhism, Pure Land Buddhism and Nichiren Buddhism are just a few of the many that have roots in Mahayana Buddhism.

Vajrayana

Vajrayana Buddhism and Tibetan Buddhism are sometimes confused. Despite this, Tibetan Buddhism does include the tantric elements from Vajrayana, although it uses practices from many different Buddhist orders. Vajrayana is closer to the Mahayana tradition that the Theravadan.

Vajrayana is distinguished from other schools of Buddhism by the fact that, in addition to meditation and other spiritual techniques, it also uses these to improve Buddhist practice. Vajrayana Buddhists use both Mahayana and Theravadan spiritual texts as well as Buddha Tantras, and other Buddhist texts.

The idea behind Vajrayana Buddhist tantras is to make it clear through the pleasures of life that you are an enlightened person. It recognizes that each person is on a different path to spiritual awakening and that everyone has different ways of reaching it. Instead of living a life of temporary pleasures and chasing after them, this pleasure-seeking energy can be used to help you achieve spiritual awakening.

As you can see there are many orders of Buddhism. The various schools also evolve into offshoots to serve the different cultures Buddhism touches.

Chapter 8: Philosophy Continued: Karma & Death & Rebirth And The Problematic Emotions

To begin any religious or spiritual journey, it is important to understand philosophical concepts. We can now explore the philosophical aspects and meaning of Buddhism once we have an understanding of The Three Jewels as well as The Four Noble Truths.

Karma

Literally translated, "karma" in Sanskrit means action. According to Buddhist teachings, karma is the motivation or intention behind one's actions. This means that what one gives will be returned. This principle can be reinterpreted in a variety of ways, including "you get what your give" and "what goes around comes about."

Karma encourages kindness, helping others and encouraging compassion. It is believed that happiness will come when you make it possible for others to have happiness. Your suffering could also be a result of suffering you have done in the past.

For those studying Buddhist theories, karma can take time to manifest itself. This is one of the most difficult concepts. In today's world, where one can see instant results for their actions, this is particularly true. Buddhist teachings also explain that past actions can lead to present-life results. However, the idea of karma ties actions and outcomes together and cannot be broken.

There are four rules to karma.

1. The results will mirror the cause. Also, if you cause suffering in someone else, you will also suffer. Positive actions will lead to happiness.

2. All results can be traced back towards a cause. Actions and results are interrelated. You cannot have one without another.

3. The results of an action are not lost once it is complete. The causes and effects of actions can't appear suddenly, but the results and actions don't disappear.

4. Karma is a way to increase your chances of success. Karma is the ability to repeat a behavior or pattern that has been completed.

Positive karma is achieved by avoiding negative thoughts and actions, meditating to promote positivity and seeking purification. Purification is about treating others with compassion, looking at past actions or how we might have hurt others, vowing not to repeat them, and practicing

Buddhism through reading texts, mantras, and any other motivational activities.

Death and Rebirth

One of the most distinctive features of Buddhist teachings is their approach to death and the beyond. Many religions consider death a final event. Buddhism, however, suggests that death is a series of events. It is often described as a series visions.

The death process ends and one is left in an intermediate state known as "bardo." Karmic processes control how long this state lasts, but a being can experience it for up to 49 consecutive days. This experience can be either pleasant or painful depending on one's karma.

The stage of rebirth follows bardo. This is not to be confused with the idea of reincarnation. Rebirth, also called "re-becoming" and "repeated deaths," means that an individual is always changing. However, reincarnation refers to an immortal soul who opposes the matter it assumes.

The Problematic Emotions

There are three elements that make up Buddhism's feeling aggregate. These are:

1. Pleasant - When we feel an attachment to an object

2. Unpleasant: When we feel aversion or hatred towards an object.

3. Neutral - When we don't feel any attachment to an object and are not concerned about it.

Buddhism's fundamental practice is to try to dismantle the ideas that give rise these labels. This means that if something is unpleasant, we should investigate the causes. Let's be open-minded about everything. We must also avoid the trap of limiting objects, people, or events to a narrow set of labels.

Aversion and anger are two of the most problematic emotions. These are their definitions:

-Aversion: The desire to be separate from an object or person.

Anger: The inability to resist the presence of an object or person, or the desire for harm. Sometimes anger is just an amplified version of aversion.

Buddhist teachings encourage patience and tolerance in order to overcome anger, aversion, or hatred. Although you might need to examine the causes of your anger and aversion, it is important to address them rather than ignore them.

Attachment is another negative emotion. It is a feeling that you are not able to leave someone or something. When attachment is exacerbated, addiction can occur. These pitfalls can be avoided by seeking wisdom and reflection to determine if the attachment is worth the negative emotions that it creates.

Buddhists are advised to avoid the following negative emotions: guilt, depression, fear, low self-esteem, and fear.

Chapter 9: Buddhist Worship

Buddhist devotees can worship in their homes or in a public temple. Many gurus recommend going to the temple to worship with other devotees.

A shrine is a place where a Buddhist devotee can set up at home. It could be in one room or in an area. The shrine usually includes a statue or effigy of Buddha, an incense torch and several candles.

A Buddhist Temple does not have a specific structure or layout. They come in many sizes and shapes. The most well-known are the Buddhist pagodas in Japan and China. Another common Buddhist structure is the Stupa. It is a stone structure that was built over the relics or replicas of Buddha's teachings.

Traditional Buddhist temples are designed to represent the elements of air, fire and water. The square foundation represents the earth, while the square top symbolises wisdom. A Buddhist temple may contain a Buddha image or statue.

Mantras

One word, one syllable or one phrase can all be considered a mantra. You can say the mantra once, or you can repeat it repeatedly. It can be spoken aloud, or just in your head. Mantras have been believed to have profound spiritual effects on those who use them.

Prayer aids

Prayer beads are used by many Buddhist devotees to indicate the number of times a mantra has been repeated. You may also see prayer wheels with mantras. While the prayer wheel spins, you will need to repeat the mantra. You can carry a small prayer or you can keep it with you.

Sacred Mandala

The Mandala is one of the most important visual articles in Tibetan Buddhism. It is symbolic of the entire universe. Mandalas can be found as scrolls or paintings on walls. You can also create Mandalas on top of tables by using colored sands. Mandalas can be made using colored sands to create vivid images in the mind of skilled Buddhists.

The mandala represents the imaginary palace that Buddhists meditate in. Each object in the palace has a particular significance. Each object in the palace represents a specific aspect of wisdom, or reminds the meditating individual of a driving principle. The mandala's purpose is to help transform an ordinary mind into a more enlightened one. Mandalas are also thought to help with healing.

Chapter 10: Reincarnation: Why is it

Important in Buddhism?

Death is only an impermanent end to an unpermanent existence.

One can recall past lives through powerful meditation. This ability will allow you to see your life in a new way.

Karma and Reincarnation offer a plausible explanation of inequality. This explains why some people are born wealthy and others are poor, and why some children are healthy while others are disabled. This may seem like a hard pill to swallow for some.

Most major Indian religions believe in the cycle, which is commonly known as "samsara," or "wandering". However, Buddhism has a slightly different view of our place in this cycle. Hinduism focuses a lot of its philosophy on the soul, or "atman," as the core of our being. Buddhism, however, rejects the notion of soul or self. We will soon be discussing in detail the illusion that we have no soul or self. Although Buddhists see samsara primarily as a painful cycle that causes suffering, it is important to remember that every lifetime, regardless of how difficult, doesn't lead to damnation. It's a temporary opportunity to make a difference in one's life. This is one of the key differences between Buddhism and other religions, especially those that believe in eternal damnation in hell.

Your birth condition will determine the lessons you must learn during your lifetime. A person might be born wealthy because it is important to him to learn the importance of generosity. Or, a person could be born poor to teach him the value of hardwork.

Skeptics often ask this question: How can it explain why the world is so much more populated today than it was a few decades ago, if our souls never really die, and if we are continually reborn in every lifetime?

The human realm is just one of many realms. We may find ourselves in another realm after we die. There are lower realms and heavenly realms. There are animal realms as well as ghostly realms. Also, it is possible for beings from other realms to be reborn in the human realm. You could have been living in another realm before being reborn in this world. Understanding that we constantly move between different realms allows us to have a deeper empathy and respect for other beings.

According to Buddhist teachings, there are six realms into which sentient beings can be spawned. These are the three higher realms that include demigods, gods, and humans and the three lower realms that include hungry ghosts and hell. The realms can sometimes be viewed as five. Demigods and god realms are one and the same. This would make the human realm second highest.

If you have not reached Nirvana, Buddhahood, or gotten very good karma, the best thing to do is be reborn into the realms of gods. This realm is, however, a heavenly one. It is believed that this realm is full of joy, luxury, and easy living. This can lead to bad karma. If one who is born into the godly realm neglects their spirituality and isn't careful, it's very likely that they will be in a lower realm.

Our human realm is plagued with suffering and misfortune but it is still considered a very fortunate outcome of one's karmic performance. Humans are more sentient than animals and have greater freedom and independence of thought. This gives us ample opportunities to improve our karma. Animals suffer greatly because they are ruled by instincts that they don't have control over.

The last two realms are, of course, the most harsh. The realm of hungry ghosts is where those who are born will experience extreme hunger, thirst, and cravings. It is said that their existence as invisible, subtle beings causes them great suffering. This is still a far cry from the hellish realm reserved for those who have accumulated significant bad karma. This realm is described in many traditions and texts. It includes multiple levels of scorching and freezing, as well as realms of torture, great pain, and other things.

You might be wondering how one escapes these realms. This is because there is little awareness and no free will to do good karma. The demerit one gets from bad karma has a course and eventually runs out. Individuals will receive punishment in hellish realms and time according to their level of wrongdoing. A person will die after receiving this punishment and will be reborn in a higher realm where they can either move up or continue to suffer, depending on how they behave. Keep in mind that Buddhism does not say anything is permanent and that everyone can end their suffering cycle.

You can see that Buddhism does not believe in eternal damnation. One will eventually rise up in the ranks and be given the chance to do better. Although technically it is possible to remain in the lower realms for an indefinite time, that will be up to the individual. While many of the rebirths into human realms can be very painful and difficult for people, they should remember that, unlike animals, they are able to fully commit to their karmic outcome and greatly accelerate the accumulation good karma.

There might be questions that you still have about these realms. It might be tempting to wonder if the lack of free will in lower realms implies that karma cannot get worse, or if there is a way to make it better. This assumption is based on the fundamental question of free will. Simply put, there are multiple realms below the human realm that are more evil than the human. This is mainly to account for different levels of evil karma people acquire and not because animals and hungry ghosts are capable of doing evil deeds that can lead them to be reborn in a lower realm. Buddhists believe that animals and lower-level creatures are equally incapable of doing wrong as they are of doing good. Animals kill because they have to, and not because they want or follow an ideology. Animals and lower-beings have to live their lives and wait for their bad luck to end. Based on your karma, it is how high you are reborn in the higher, more conscious realms. Animals are generally not able to be reborn into hell or hungry ghosts. They can choose to remain in their current realm or move up when they die.

As you can see only humans and those above them can be as wicked as they can, which could lead to them being sent to hell. A person who is negligent and causes harm to animals during their lifetime could be reincarnated in the realm of animals if they do not take care. If the person murders others for money and is careless, their rebirth could pass all realms and take them to hell. There, they will face the appropriate punishments and suffering based on the severity of their crimes.

The Tibetan Book of the Dead

People who are familiar with Buddhism may have also heard of the "Tibetan Book of the Dead." This piece of literature deals in detail with the idea of rebirth, death, and how to contact them. However, it is not as frightening as it sounds. Although the Book of the Dead doesn't contain any instructions about how to contact wandering spirits or raise them, it does provide some guidance.

It is a complicated story about how this book got to its current form in West. But, it is far more important than its subject matter and origins. This "book" has undergone many revisions, additions, reinterpretations and adaptations over the years. However, the most important part of the story is its origins and subject matter.

Bardo Thodol focuses on two main topics. The first is that it teaches how to recognize signs of death and prepare for it in a ritualistic way. Bardo Thodol, which is a type of instruction manual, can also be used to guide the dying and the recently deceased through the transition from death to rebirth. This is the murky, intermediate state between death & rebirth and where the dying person's consciousness will experience many valuable experiences.

Bardo Thodol explains in detail the visions and other experiences the dying person will have during and after death. These instructions are intended to be used in the same way they were intended. They should be read to the person in question both during and after death in order to help them to process their experiences and attain liberation.

This guide of death describes the intermediate state in terms of three main bardos, or phases. Bardo Thodol explains each of these in detail. It also includes everything one will experience in this dream-like state. Both unsettling and peaceful experiences will be intertwined throughout the entire process, creating a state of mind that alternates between terror and peace.

The first bardo starts when one's consciousness has separated from the body at death. This is the phase where one meets the "clear light" of reality, which in a way represents liberation. The instructions of Bardo Thodol are read aloud to the unconscious to encourage and guide the deceased to fully embrace the experience. At this point, the emphasis is on defeating the self. This phenomenon must be perceived by the passing individual through compassion and love for all living creatures. They must also understand that "the clear lights" are not on their account and must let go all self-centered notions of importance. These factors, along with one's life and accumulated Karma, are often what keep most people from liberation in the first bardo. The second stage of this phase is called the "secondary clear lights" and it is where those who failed to attain liberation during the first stage will be able to get their second chance. Their consciousness will travel into the next phase if they fail again.

The second bardo is reserved for those who have not achieved full realization or liberation in the first. These people are believed to be many, because they have the same spiritual commitment and meditation required for the first bardo. Tibetan Buddhists believe that the second bardo lasts for two weeks and has two stages. This phase is said to include many Buddha forms and peaceful deities. Each day, one Buddha form will greet the traveling consciousness. This bardo will determine the next steps. It is determined by the way one has lived their lives and how their consciousness interacts to each of them.

The second week is where the experience turns from the frightening to the beholding. These wrathful deities will appear in very evil forms and can be extremely threatening. The passing person is encouraged to confront the monsters calmly and confidently in their hearts and eventually realize that they are not real. These beings may be peaceful deities hiding behind their frightening facades. The deceased is taught through Bardo Thodol that they must understand this and not flee from the deities' wrath in order to achieve liberation. Failure to complete this bardo will result in one's consciousness being banished down to the third stage.

The third bardo is where the experiences escalate further. In this instance, Yamantaka, who was regarded as the conqueror or lord of death, appears to be the consciousness of the deceased. This terrifying deity, who terrorizes the beholder, will serve as a judge of one's life. The dead go through this phase, where they are forced to confront their bad and good karma. They are expected to accept all of it. The goal for the dead, according to Bardo Thodol is to embrace all these deeds and fully realize the Lord Of Death and all his demons and then meditate on the clear light. This is the last chance to attain enlightenment and freedom from rebirth. The only remaining option for the "soul", after this point, is to be reborn.

The realm into which one is reincarnated will depend on the journey they have taken and how they have done through the bardo stages. Even if liberation is not possible, Bardo Thodol will still give instructions to the dead in order to help them fight for a favorable rebirth.

The dream-like state bardo is a series of tests and trials that will determine whether a soul will be able to transcend the cycle of rebirth and reach enlightenment or Buddhahood. Your chances of surviving this state will be greatly affected by the life you have lived. This Tibetan Buddhist tradition is intended to offer every person a chance for a better tomorrow.

We arrive back in the realm where all things are living and existing. However, there is an important concept and set beliefs that defines Buddhism as a whole and not just the Tibetan traditions.

What is Reincarnation?

Reincarnation refers to the continuation of the soul even after death. According to Hinduism, the soul moves into another body when you die. This depends on what your actions were. If you have done good, good karma, your soul will move into a better body after your death. Your soul will become a worse being if you have bad karma.

What is the Buddhist way of Rebirth?

Many new Buddhist students are misled into believing that Rebirth or Reincarnation means the same thing. They don't. Reincarnation is not a concept that Buddhism accepts. The immortality of the soul is the basis for reincarnation. Buddhists believe that the soul disintegrates into different elements of nature just like the body. Buddhism doesn't believe in the transmigration or reincarnation of the soul. They believe in the continuity of good intentions (karma) from one life into another. On the other hand, your bad karma creates ignorance and unsatisfied wants that cause rebirth. This is something that occurs from moment to moment (also afterwards death) and can also be called self-imprisonment and suffering. You can stop rebirth.

According to Buddhists, what happens after death?

A nice Zen story is that of the Zen master asking the disciple.

"What happens after death master?"

The master replied, "I don't know."

The disciple said: "How is that possible?" Aren't you a master?"

The master replied, "Yes, but you're not a dead one."

You should be aware that the Buddha did not like speculating about the future or the beginning of the world. He knew that no one can know for certain when death will occur and how it all began. Buddha did not consider himself to be a God or a godly creature. He believed that it was better to face the daily problems and improve the lives of those around you than speculate about what the future holds.

Even Buddha might have said "That's not very important at all" because Buddhism emphasizes the present moment. This is the only time you can make a difference in your life and live a happy life.

Did you know that your body can change all its cells in seven years. After that, you become a completely new person. Buddha once stated that "Every moment you're born, decay, then die" was referring to the illusion of "self", which is constantly renewing itself. Talk about the possibility of carrying something from one life to the next after death. Nothing is ever carried from one moment to another. When chemicals and neurotransmitters interact with one another, your emotions and thoughts change constantly. Your hair falls out and your skin cells grow new ones. Even though you don't know it, your face and body are constantly changing. According to the Buddha, your "permanent self" (your personality, consciousness, or identity) is an illusion created by your thoughts, concepts, beliefs, values, and senses. Ask me: Where is the child you were as a child? What are your thoughts about the monsters under your bed? Or your favorite activities like playing on the carpet with your blocks? Is there a little fragile body there? Beyond your memories and name, what is the link between you and that child? Every second is a rebirth.

Two constants in the world are change and death. Meditation will help you to see that death is not something you fear. You will also be less concerned about the future. Instead, you will be anchored in the moment as it is everything you've ever had or will have. You will cease suffering from others and realize that the idea of a permanent metaphysical "I", is a lie.

Forms appear and disappear every second, just like clouds in the sky. This is true for both psychical and physical forms. Did you know that 99.9999999999999% is empty space in an atom? According to physics, 99.9999999999999% of the atom is empty space. Everything else you perceive as solid also almost completely empty. You are almost completely empty. Oxygen makes up about 65% of your body, while water makes up the majority. We also have a lot of energy in our bodies. Are we solid?

The Earth moves around the Sun at sixty seven thousand miles an hour. This is not counting the speed at which it surface moves and the speed at which our Solar system rotates around the center of the galaxy at four hundred ninety-ninety thousand miles an hour. Yet, we see it as if it is stationary. It is all illusion.

There are radio waves and WiFi waves in air, the Internet and Earth's electromagnetic field. We can't see and sense many of these phenomena. Quantum physics even suggests that the entire Universe is a big hologram, and that it's just an extension of a two-dimensional surface. However, physicists know that the Universe cannot lose the information. It must be accessible to us. This is what Buddha stated long before quantum physics research began: there is no information or energy that is lost in the world. The "spirit" - the energy that animates and animates you - can never be lost. This is why death cannot be applied to real life. This life is like a wave. At some point, it will return to its ocean home. Most suffering stems from our perceptions of reality and ourselves. Meditation deeply will help you to see that false ideas such as existence, non-existence, and coming and going are false. When you are able to touch the reality, "suchness" or Tathata - the ultimate existence – will become apparent. Obsessing about death is a sign that you have wrong perceptions.

Buddhism talks about Nirvana, the end of all suffering and the ultimate goal of Buddhism. It is often called "the ability to remove misunderstanding". You can eliminate the fear of death and other negative perceptions through Nirvana. There is a transformation, a continuation but there is no death. You can't be anything and then become nothing. With constant meditation practice and the following of Buddha's principles, you can get rid of ideas like death.

According to me, when you die, the last few seconds of your life are spent experiencing yourself as an unattached consciousness. It's clear that death is an illusion. This is similar to the form that is vanishing, the one that you have been stubbornly identifying with. You feel like everything is fine and that you are just returning to the place you came from.

The thing I love about Buddhism is its refusal to recognize eternal damnation. I have never believed that humans could be condemned (or sent to hell by a supreme being), for their sins. There is no way to redeem them. It is the most cruel and sadistic idea ever created, if you really think about it. Even the most horrific horror stories and movies seem to be like "Casper the Friendly Ghost", a popular prospect.

Despite being Catholic, I went to church and confessed my sins. I also spent a few years as an acolyte while I was a child. I couldn't believe that a loving Father would accept such cruelty, even when it came to the most serious criminals. I believed that even the most harmful "energy" should eventually be depleted, as with the energy derived from good deeds. It seemed to me that unchanging eternity was not possible (maybe my Buddhist mind was at work). This was not justice. I spent hours talking to my parents, priests and monks and sat in libraries reading many Christian and Muslim theological books. Because that belief didn't fit with my vision of the world or my concept of God, I struggled to find the answers. I couldn't believe that any supremely intelligent, loving, and loving being could allow eternal hell to exist. It was a strange concept to me. The few answers I found ("that's God's mystery") said that we were the ones who would be going away from God's purifying love. He could not save us if our souls were wretched, and He wouldn't allow us to lose our free will. It was a scene in which a father watches his son set on fire with gasoline and then jump out of a skyscraper's windows. I thought it looked like this. The father said, "If he wishes to jump, let him!" - he believes that he has free will. He can't commit suicide, or else I would have made him slave. Seems legit? Perhaps to some, but not me.

My view is purely personal and I don't want to offend. However, I did find a few Catholic priests who believed hell was empty because God's love was too strong to allow this kind of cruelty.

There are many (looooots) of them! There are many Buddhist sects. Each has its own beliefs. But, the majority of them believe that there is an existence in multiple realms of this universe. This includes hell, which is filled with depraved men and then a dimension of hungry spirits (similar to Western ghost stories about lonely spirits who can't find peace). Human beings, Bodhisattvas, who are enlightened beings that have been destined to remain on this planet to teach others, Pratyekas, who are Buddha's followers, and Sravkas, and Sravkas -enlightened beings (Budhas), and Sravkas -s.

You've probably noticed that there is also a concept called hell - but it's not permanent. You can remain there for thousands of year, or even eons depending on your actions and intentions - but eventually you are cleansed. Many believe that Karma can make someone reborn as a human being again if they have better Karma. They will need to go through their past mistakes to understand the Noble Eightfold Path and then they will be given the Karma from their previous life. This will allow them to end the continuous cycle of rebirth, which is ineffective and causes pain, and eventually, they will find the peace and bliss of Nirvana.

Personally, I believe that these realms should not be taken literally or religiously. These realms can be difficult to understand and investigate in modern times. Buddhism is all about rationality. Buddhism teaches more than this. It teaches that no soul (anatta), can transmigrate to another body. One cannot literally be reborn like a cat or an annoying spider. .

You are not an individual being with a separate mind, but are one with the Universe. You can imagine yourself as a limitless, unlimited space. It is you. Rebirth is a dance between forms appearing and disappearing, another illusion and another shift. Yet, you are not one of them. You are connected with all things. It's difficult to grasp until you start meditating deeply, and follow the Buddha's teachings. Human beings cannot speak the truth, just the words that express it. These words can often be misguided or futile.

You should know that Buddha taught more than eighty thousand lessons throughout his life. He also adjusted his teachings to the spiritual and mental abilities of his listeners and students. These realms were probably created as parables, similar to the Biblical ones Jesus preached so frequently. These universal images were created to help people better understand "the nature" of things. These images were also meant to be used as a moral example. I can see that the simple rural Asian settlers of 500 BC were afraid of being reborn animals. This probably prevented them from acting as animals and allowed them peace. This helped them to learn other important truths about human relationships and life.

No matter what belief one holds in hell or heaven, or continuous rebirths in these realms up to Nirvana until that point, I believe they should be considered psychological conditions we are pushing ourself into, due to our good and bad karma. Furthermore, each realm contains all other realms. As a human being, you might be listening to your bodily needs, and acting as if you were a wild animal (sex, porn addiction, drinking, etc.). You could be hungry for fame, love, popularity, relationships or love. Either you are pushing yourself further into hell by being selfish or you could follow the noble path to compassion and meditation and find calm and happiness, just like the Buddha. You would also need to be an enlightened being (Buddha) to understand how the hell on Earth or a state where you are hungry for something in order to help your principles.

You should also be able to see how animals act more humanely and morally than you used to.

There's more to it when it comes down to the afterlife or karma. But this e-book is short and informative. If I were to go into detail about Zen Buddhism or Tibetan Buddhism, it would take me at most a few hundred pages. So that you (and a few hundred million other Buddhists) can understand what I believe, I have briefly explained the idea.

You can also read the Tibetan "Bardo Thodol", which is translated by Walter Evans Wentz or the Tibetans. It describes the experiences that consciousness after death is free from its human body. It's strikingly similar with many near-death stories of people who survived serious accidents (light in a tunnel, overview of one's entire life, floating above oneself, presence of loving and good energy, etc.). It can also be used with the Kabbalistic conceptions and Taoism as well as the Egyptian Book of the Dead. However, it is not consistent with traditional Buddhism. You are responsible for your own learning and should be able to approach the knowledge and philosophy in your own way.

It can be your belief or not. But Buddha says that you should only accept it if it makes sense to YOU personally and you are able to find the truth within it. Despite your feelings, it's one of the few concepts that makes sense to me. It gives me hope.

Chapter 11: Building Mindful and Meaningful Relationships

Never have you heard the expression "No man is an island", Because we all have some connection, it is true. It would be foolish to try to isolate ourselves from others. We should strive to make our relationships as meaningful and mindful as possible. What is a mindful relationship? A mindful relationship is one you cultivate and nurture; you get back as much as you put in.

At a young age, relationships are taught. Our parents are the first relationship we have in this life. We learn from our parents the principles of give and take. We form our first social charter with our parents about how we should behave in society. Many of their positive traits and their flaws are mirrored by us.

Even if your upbringing wasn't the greatest, it is not a reason to lose heart. We can always learn from our mistakes and improve our relationship approach. You must take immediate action if you are aware of a problem in your approach. This can be done by surround yourself with positive people who will support your growth.

Although toxic people cannot always be avoided, it is important to do our best to avoid them. We need people we can trust and to whom we can talk freely without fear of being judged. People who have lived through the fire are usually the most compassionate and non-judgmental. These brave souls have the ability to share their wisdom and experience from hard work. These battle-tested, experienced individuals can help you get up in times of trouble.

Eckhart Tolle, a Buddhist philosopher and expert on relationships, says there are only two types of relationships: those that "enlighten" or those that feed an addiction. Toxic relationships are those that feed an addiction and not help us improve ourselves. To avoid this, we need to let go of any ego or selfish desires and seek out relationships that are non-judgmental and accepting.

The most important thing about any relationship in your life is that you have no control over it. You cannot control your girlfriend or spouse's actions as much as you can control the neighbors down the street. However, we can control how our temperaments are affected. Buddhism teaches that you can control your response to the stimuli of the world to live a happier life.

This is a reminder of the four noble truths that Buddha teaches us. The Buddha says the world is full suffering. To learn how to alleviate it, I must first admit it to myself and then learn not to be influenced by it. This is how we can end the cycle of pain and disappointment. These principles are equally applicable to relationships.

Chapter 12: Let's practice!

Practical application is the only way to apply all the information about the teachings of Buddha, the path to Enlightenment and other related topics. Once you've shown an interest in Buddhism, I'll show you how to apply the teachings of Buddha in your daily life. This will help you get on the path to happiness and enlightenment. We will expand our knowledge about meditation and chanting in the next chapter. These are the two most important daily practices of Buddhism. I'll also share some Buddhism tips to help you deal with the multitude of emotions that we experience every day.

As we have discussed in previous chapters, Nirvana is only possible through compassion and egolessness. This chapter will help you gain a better understanding about Buddhism and how it can be applied in your everyday life. It will also show you how to cultivate compassion for people you don't know and those you love.

Daily Meditation

Although we've all heard about the benefits meditation has, I bet you are still curious as to how to meditate. Meditation is not just deep breathing and chanting. Meditation is intended to calm the mind, reduce stress and help us develop healthy habits. It's okay if it doesn't feel like that first time. The process is gradual.

You will eventually be so skilled at meditation that you can easily drift into your peaceful place, no matter where it is. These tips for beginners are great to get you started.

You need to find a place: It is important that you have a quiet and clean space for meditation. This allows you to clear your mind more easily. Clear and free space is conducive to a clear and free mind. This is why you won't be able to think clearly about your work if your space is messy.

You can use music or not: Music is up to you. Traditional Buddhist teachings discourage the use of music in meditation because it makes you rely on someone else to achieve tranquility. But don't let this stop you. Some people find that music can help them block out distractions. Be careful about the music you choose as it could distract from your focus.

Relax: Meditation is as much about the body and mind as it is about the mind. Having the right posture can help increase its effectiveness. Your back should be straight, whether you are sitting on the ground or in a chair. You should also have your neck, shoulders and facial muscles relaxed. This is so your body can relax and clear your mind.

Time is relative. It doesn't matter how busy you may be, you still have time to meditate. Beginners should meditate for three to five minutes each. It is more difficult to remain focused for longer periods than five minutes. This is all to help you clear your mind and stay focused for a time. Meditation is more effective when you can focus for a shorter time without distractions.

Frequency: How frequently should you meditate? The simple answer is yes. Buddhism encourages meditation and you should practice it every day. Don't limit your practice to once per day. You can meditate whenever you have some quiet time to clear your head. It could happen once in the morning, once at lunch, and once at night. Or it could be 10 times per hour with short breaks. You can do whatever you like, but be consistent in your search for tranquility.

Body: Some people meditate cross-legged while others prefer to meditate on a couch, chair or the edge of their bed. It doesn't matter where you meditate, ensure that your body is grounded. This means that you should sit on the ground or with furniture. If you are sitting in a chair, ensure that your feet are planted on the ground. This will help you to be rooted with the Earth. Some prefer to hold their fingers in a tight squeeze while resting their thighs lightly on their thighs. Others prefer to keep their hands flat. If you want to show gratitude, your palms should be facing up. However, if your palms face down, your hands should remain flat. For beginners, it is best to hold your hands flat with your palms facing down. Meditation is best done in a calm and open mind.

Breathing: If you are unable to listen to music, meditation can be done by focusing on your breath. You can also focus on your breathing to quickly find relief from stressful situations. These are some breathing tips:

Keep your breathing in tune, but continue to breathe normally. (No need for exaggerated breathing)

Focusing on only two aspects of breathing can help you to increase your energy levels if you're tired or to keep your mind from wandering if you get distracted. When meditating, you should be focusing on the act of breathing in and out and the sensation of your abdomen contracting when you breathe. These two aspects will keep your mind focused and prevent you from drifting.

Your breathing is an important part of your life. Our minds are not going to shut off, so it is important that we can gently guide our thoughts back. You can test your meditation skills by judging how well your mind can guide it back to the task after it has wandered.

Meditation can help you find life-changing happiness. To reap its benefits we need to make a habit of it. Meditation is not only a spiritual practice, but it can also be a healing tool. Meditation is more than a stress reliever. It can also help you to stay grounded, ease your physical pain, and calm your emotions. Meditation can help you focus and achieve your goals. This can help those suffering from anxiety or depression to move beyond the stressors of the diseases and overcome the obstacles that are presented to them. It will also help you regain your life. You will notice the clutter build up in your life if you meditate for a few consecutive days.

When that happens, you will know it is time to meditate again. These feelings can be controlled by meditating daily, even for just 5-10 minutes.

Finding everyday happiness

As we have discussed, Buddhism teaches that "self" and "ego" are the two most important things to let go of in order to achieve true happiness. How do we do this? These are some tips you can apply in your daily life to let go ego and get closer to inner peace.

You can meditate by finding some quiet time. No matter what your situation, you should make an effort to find some quiet time each day. Even if meditation is not your thing, there are still other ways to relax and release stress. You can read quietly and let your mind wander. Then, you can explore those thoughts using a journal. Every day, take 15 minutes to yourself. This can include ignoring the world's problems and shutting off the outside world. If done mindfully, it can be a form meditation to do the dishes. Sometimes life can be stressful. A little peace and quiet can make a big difference in a stressful day.

Do something nice every day: It is important to do something kind for others each and every day. Compassion for others is a fundamental principle of Buddhism. You will find the happiness you are looking for in genuine gestures. You don't need to do a lot of nice gestures towards your friends, family, co-workers, or strangers. You can do something as simple as unloading the dishwasher to your wife, or getting a cup of coffee for the coworker next door. It can be difficult to find the time to perform larger gestures when you work full-time and have family and friends. Even small acts of kindness, such as the ones listed above, can make a big difference in someone's day and your own. Even if it's only 5-10 minutes, the feeling of euphoria you get from a stranger is priceless. You can make someone's day by doing the same thing for them.

Don't forget generosity: Generosity should not be forgotten. Instead, it's people who become so attached to themselves and think badly about others that they neglect to be generous. It is impossible to predict what the homeless man on the street will do with your money, but it is not a reason to stop helping. Your self-worth will be elevated by your generosity. Similar to the previous idea, you should try. Even if you can only give a few hours or a little money, you will be amazed at how much your self-worth and self-esteem are raised by generosity. It doesn't necessarily mean that you have to give up your life in order to help others. Instead of focusing on yourself, try to think about the people around you.

Concentrate on your strengths. We lose nothing if we try to change things that are beyond our control. Instead, be proud of your strengths and work to improve yourself. Start with your strongest strength, and you can open up your mind to other people as you go.

Pray forgiveness. As we have discussed, Buddhism says that holding on to emotions can keep us from real happiness. Be open to the injustices done to you by others and yourself. Although this is one of the most difficult to do, it will be the most rewarding. People can carry so much stress with them if they don't forgive others who are doing the right thing, even if it is for their own benefit.

All things pass. Take the ups, downs and joys of life with you. You will find the light eventually, even if you are going through a lot. Keep your eyes on the positives and remember that storms do not last forever.

These six tips will help you to increase your self-worth and reduce stress. They will also help you to be mentally and physically stronger.

How to deal with anxiety, anger, jealousy, and developing love

Buddhism's teachings are meant to help us find greater happiness in our lives, but we also believe that life isn't always pleasant. Therefore, we need to acknowledge and address our negative feelings.

Anxiety refers to a feeling of being overwhelmed and making us want to hide in our rooms for the rest of your life. Anxiety can make it difficult to find inner peace. Meditation, the most sought-after route to happiness and tranquility in Buddhism, can be a great option for those suffering from severe anxiety disorders. Meditation can help you focus on your own well-being and calm your anxious mind. It can also slow down the anxiety and panic that runs through your body. These tips can help you combat anxiety if meditation doesn't work.

Rewind: Take a moment to reflect on your life. Ask the hard questions to determine what you want from your life. Is it worth the high-powered job? Do you still get the same joy from working long hours, earning great money, and driving a fancy car?

People change and evolve all the time, and priorities can shift. Sometimes it's as simple as realizing that you aren't doing what you should. Other times, such realizations can lead to nervous breakdowns, high blood pressure, high stress and high blood sugar. Take a moment to evaluate your life and identify the root cause of anxiety.

Find role models: Look for someone who lives the life you desire and look up to them. You can learn from their strategies and apply them to your own life. Role models can be helpful in all aspects of your life, including your home, business, and goals. This will help you to not feel overwhelmed by trying to figure everything out all by yourself.

You can't control everything. This is the root cause of crippling anxiety. It doesn't matter if your family is happy, what the weather is like, or how your family reacts to world events. Anxiety attacks can result from trying too hard to control everything. You can't control everything in your life.

Only you can control your actions. Take a moment to meditate, and then relax.

Help others: This shifts your focus. It's not about you. Sometimes it can be very difficult to see the suffering of others. It makes you more compassionate and helps you appreciate your life. Some anxiety can be severe, such as severe anxiety, while others can be mild to moderate. You can change the latter by focusing on what you have and recognizing what is most important in your life. Sometimes, all you need to do is look at how others live to help put your problems in perspective.

Recognize who you are. Don't let the "perfect" life people live on social media fool you. The idea that we are all one person makes it seem like we all are searching for the "perfect" life. Realize that there is no such thing. True happiness is found in living a meaningful life that isn't always perfect. To gain a better perspective on your life, and to see how you are doing, take a break from social networking.

Mindfulness: Although it may seem counterintuitive, let negative thoughts seep into the brain and throughout your body. Take care of each thought individually, helping to resolve the problem. Although you may feel anxious, frustrated, or scared about the thoughts plaguing your mind, take the time to separate them. This will help remove them from your mind and worries. Mindfulness reduces stress levels, which makes it easier to live your life the way that you want.

Next we will deal with anger. This is the emotion we experience far too often. You can begin to feel less anger with the practice of Buddhism. You can control your anger by practicing the practice of Buddhism. Mindfulness can be used to reduce anxiety and depression. It can also help you manage anger, calm down, and help you get through stressful situations. These 8 tips can help you cope with anger.

Undisputed life: We all know that life is never easy. There will be good and bad times. And there will also be times when we feel indifferent. This is how the cookie crumbles. Remember that everyone is in this together, and that anger does not solve problems. When life isn't going as planned, it can be difficult to overcome anger. This is especially true if you look at the success of others. You can get back to Earth by remembering that life can be messy.

Patience is the antithesis of anger, and it cancels out anger. It is weakness to allow our emotions to get the best of us. But, fighting our anger with patience, is another level strength, mental strength. Don't worry if you're impatient. There will be times in your life when patience can't help you. It is about knowing when those times are, and when you can take a deep breath and think it over. Then proceed cautiously. You can be patient with small things that might get you upset, such as waiting in line at the store or your two-year old not putting their toys away. You'll be able to practice patience daily and you will soon be able use it more when bigger problems arise.

Analyse: Understand that anger is a enemy, not a friend. Don't let it control your life or make you "angry all of the time". You can find out the root cause of your anger, and then explore how to stop it from coming back. Although there are many reasons for anger, you may still harbor anger from multiple sources. However, one issue will trigger your anger, no matter how minor or major. The root cause of the anger sudden outburst is what you should be looking at.

Be mindful. Develop mindfulness, awareness, meditation relief, and mindfulness. Clear your mind and get as focused as possible. This is especially important when you are going through difficult times. Instead of running from negative thoughts and running away, face them head-on. You can tackle a big work project or mountains of paperwork mindfully. This will keep you from having negative thoughts and feelings.

Learn from your enemies. When people who have been wronged are able to see who is responsible, they often seek revenge. While revenge may seem good at first, it soon becomes a habitual response that leaves us with a bitter taste. Find out what useful tips you can learn from them. Stop seeking revenge on your enemies. You will feel better about yourself and the people around you if you practice forgiveness.

Impermanence: Recognize that tomorrow is uncertain and that life is too precious to be angry. You can escape the concept of impermanence through Buddhism by reaching Nirvana. You cannot escape impermanence, which is what you can't escape such as death. You cannot escape from the fact that nothing lasts forever. To let go of your anger, you have to realize that everyone around you and the entire world are constantly changing. This is something to keep in mind when you feel angry. What angers you today may not seem so bad tomorrow.

Karma: We discussed how compulsive behaviors can be created by repetitive actions. You can change your bad habits and create good ones. Karma in Buddhism is more harsh than the old adage "what goes around, comes around"; karma is caused by anger and hatred. If anger or hatred takes control of your life, you are likely to fall prey to one of the 32 hells found in Buddhism. This is something you shouldn't take lightly. You can get rid of anger by taking steps to make sure it doesn't control your life. You can start with small, easy habits and work your way up until you're free.

Emptiness: Most of the time, anger is a feeling of emptyness. Often, the things that actually make us angry are so minor that we forget them quickly. You will soon realize that you were not angry about anything before you can allow yourself to get lost in your emotions. Is it worth fighting for if you can't remember what you are fighting for? Mindfulness can help you to look deeper into the reasons that led you to this point. You might feel frustrated and can use breathing techniques to help you stay grounded. Other times, it could be filled with nothing at any point. Anger that is fuelled by emptiness can be dangerous. Bring your thoughts inward to learn how you can tell the difference between 'empty' anger from true anger.

To live a happier and more fulfilled life, use these tools to combat anger and anxiety. Buddhism teaches mindfulness, which is essential to unlock your potential and that of the world around. It teaches you to let go and live a life worth living. An angry and anxious life is not one that is conscious of its well-being.

We will now discuss jealousy. Jealousy can make us anxious about our relationships with others and take away our peace of mind. Jealousy can be a very painful emotion. It is often associated with envy of others. Jealousy is when we feel that someone else's property belongs to us. This should have been our idea. Our car.

Our house. Our trip. It is very difficult to accept that it is not ours and that the world doesn't consist of us alone.

The key to overcoming jealousy is knowing that we are capable of loving everyone. Reaffirming that we are capable of loving multiple people simultaneously and equally is a must. It is important to open our hearts and love others, as well as encourage them to do so. This requires being mindful, being kind and being present to yourself. Anxiety, jealousy, anger, and envy can all be caused by focusing on the accomplishments of others instead of your own. Buddhism encourages you to look within and find the things that bring you joy. You may find the joys of life quite simple. However, kindness, generosity, and meditation can make you happier and bring you more fulfillment in your daily life.

This brings me to the meaning of love and how having our hearts open for love can help us on our way.

To develop love, you must appreciate our interconnectedness. It's compassion for others, and knowing that we share similar experiences. Start small by developing love for yourself and wanting happiness. You can bring these feelings into your own life by using loving-kindness meditation. You may find it helpful to repeat a mantra. This will remind you of your love and kindness, or help you feel calm and happy. Those feelings are then passed on to others. It starts with our closest friends, then spreads to others, then to strangers and finally to all living things. You can share the feelings of love you just established in yourself with others by picturing your love for one another. Consider the good qualities that they and you share. Bring these feelings to people you aren't as close to or who you don't feel any attachment towards. It can be difficult to bring kindness and compassion to people you dislike or hate. You can keep bringing your happiness and love to yourself and your friends, and paying attention to how you breathe. This will help you to complete the image with the person that you don't like. Once you have the final image, you can spread your feelings of compassion and love out into the world. You can also use the peace and tranquility within to help you stay grounded and keep you focused. Slowly and mindfully breathe in, and bring your attention back to the present moment. To truly feel happy, we must love ourselves and all things. Meditation using loving-kindness can help with anxiety, jealousy, anger, and other feelings. It also helps you spread love in your community and around the world.

Everyday Wisdom and Compassion

Buddhism's main teaching is that wisdom and compassion are essential for true enlightenment. Both are not compatible because wisdom is grounded in logic, while compassion is only emotional. Buddhism defines wisdom as "consciousness", or awareness of the meanings and experiences of existence. It states that compassion can be defined as being actively involved in the well-being and emotions of others. Being compassionate can make a huge difference in your life. Begin by being compassionate with yourself. People tend to be more negative about themselves than they are towards others. Recognize that mistakes are inevitable and that they will happen throughout your life. However, it doesn't mean that this should stop you from being the person you truly are. These are some ways to bring wisdom and compassion into your daily life once you've learned compassion.

Take care of the sick: Don't try to save someone you love from suffering. Instead, you should actively seek a cure for the illness. Offer them soup and medicine. Let them know that you are sharing your experiences. It's no surprise that so many people choose to work as firefighters, police officers, nurses, or doctors. Human beings are naturally inclined to help others. You can control what happens in the future by helping others who are sick or in need.

Help someone in need: Listen to and offer advice when they are going through difficult times. Recognizing these interconnected experiences is a way to find inner peace. It's natural to want others around you to support you when you're feeling down. The connection between you and those you care about, or those you don't know grows stronger when you help them. People often find that they are closer to one another in difficult times. They learn from each other's mistakes and can continue to live with greater peace and tranquility.

Repay kindness: It's important to be grateful for the kindness shown to us by others. Pay your parents for the sacrifices they have made for you, for example. This should be done with gratitude. Helping someone when they don't want it isn't helping you. There are many sacrifices that people make in life. It was a great honor to be there for them in times of need.

Be comforting for the afraid: Don't dismiss someone's cry of need. Let someone who is afraid know that things will improve. Sometimes we forget that everything will improve eventually when we are afraid. We need someone to remind this. Your life will be calmer and happier if you are there to help someone who is in pain, afraid, or just need your advice.

Consolate the grieving: Try to imagine yourself in the shoes of the grieving individual. This is an experience that can be shared by all. Everybody has experienced the pain of grieving for a loved one. Instead of being a patron, console people with active compassion.

Donate to the poor: This money goes to street panhandlers as well as charities. There are many people who ask for money and help. Many of these are often families in trouble. Put yourself in their shoes. Don't make assumptions about what they will trade for what you give. It doesn't matter what you do.

Spread Dharma: It's all about offering meaningful advice to others who are seeking it. As Buddhism is a teaching system, it is important to share the teachings with others. All negative events in our lives can be attributed to negative thoughts according to Buddhism. You can protect yourself from negative life events by practicing dharma, teaching others, and bring peace to your body, mind, and soul.

Respecting others' wishes is a sign of selflessness. Take care of others, as well as yourself. Try something that your partner likes, for example. Sometimes it can be difficult to let go of your own desires and accept the wishes of others, especially if you believe that your way is best. If it doesn't put anyone at risk, don't let your emotions get in the way of their ideas. Instead, embrace them.

Promote positivity and support others living positive, uplifting lives. It is essential to have a support system, and to encourage and support others. Positive thoughts and feelings can help you let go of negative emotions and events, and allow your mind and body the opportunity to absorb the best that the world has for you.

Nurture the destructive: If you are close to someone on a destructive path, don't reject, condemn, or dismiss them. Instead of condemning people, show them how to improve themselves. We know that if you're on a negative path with negative thoughts, then negative events will continue to happen. If you don't dismiss someone on a negative and destructive path, they will continue to follow that path. You don't have the right to abandon your life in order to cope with destructive behavior that could overtake your positive ways. However, let them know you will be there for them when they need it. You can help them learn how to improve themselves by starting with meditation and kindness. They might not be as bad as they appear and may just have lost their way.

Make use of your talents: No matter what your talent (musician or motivational speaker, architect, etc.), you can use it for good. Use your talent to inspire others and make the world a better destination. You can use your talents the way you choose, not the way others expect you to. Don't give up on your gift. Focus on the things that make you happy and practice your talents. You will be able to do good things if you feel good. Your talents can spread love and happiness to all those around you.

You can learn to unite with other people: A connection is something that is very powerful, whether it's a friendship, business relationship, or romantic one. These feelings can be used to unite others and help them take care of their relationships. It doesn't matter how many connections you make, if you don't nurture them, you won't be able to achieve tranquility or happiness. You will find fulfillment, peace, happiness and companionship in those around you who are looking for them.

Understanding non-attachment is a key issue. We are attached to our homes and cars, jobs, families, friends, pets, and family. Many materialistic possessions can strain our relationships and cause stress that can lead to overwhelm. These things should not be all-consuming. You've reached non-attachment when you can enjoy life and all it has to offer, but are still able to let it go.

Stop fearing death. Everything is temporary. This is what Buddhism teaches and something we can all see. Accept the idea of death. This does not mean that you should wait for it to come to you, but that it will eventually. Accept this reality and you will feel more open. People who face death or see it before them, and are able to accept it, find a way to live a more satisfying life. You can do the same and view death not as something to be afraid of, but as something that is inevitable. This will make it easier for everyone and everything. Look out at the world and find beauty in all that you see, touch, feel, or taste.

Living naturally means to live in a way that allows you to see the world as it really is. The world, and everything in it, is always changing (impermanence), and everything is connected to one another (interconnectedness). These two concepts will help you to see the world on a larger scale and achieve tranquility in your mind and soul.

It is important to be generous with our time and our materials. Compassion requires self-discipline and perseverance, as well as patience. It's about creating inner peace and encouraging others to live happier lives.

Chapter 13: Buddhist Traditions

Buddha advised us to not believe in any tradition simply because it is traditional. We don't have to abandon all traditions and this is one of the most generous statements ever made by a religious scholar. Other religious scholars are unaware of this tolerance for other customs and traditions. These religious leaders often advise their new converts that they give up all their traditions, customs, and culture. They don't care if they are right, wrong, or both. Buddhist missionaries have never recommended that people abandon their traditions in order to preach the Dhamma. As long as they are reasonable,

The traditions and customs should be kept within the framework of the principles of religion. To put it another way, one should not disregard religious precepts in order to keep his traditions. If they want to keep their traditions that have no religious value, they can do so as long as they don't practice them in the name religion. Even so, these religious practices should not be harmful to others or one's self.

Rituals and Rituals

They are part of traditions and customs. These are psychological aids for the people. You can still practice your religion without rituals and rites. People may consider certain rituals and rites the most important part of their religion, but they are not essential to this faith. For spiritual development and purity of mind, one should avoid such practices according to Buddha.

Festivals

Genuine Buddhists don't celebrate Buddhist festivals while drinking, smoking or by eating meat. Real Buddhists observe festivals in a different manner. Buddhists would dedicate their time to abstaining all evil powers on the day. To relieve their anxiety, they would be able to help others and practice charity. They can entertain their friends and family in a very professional manner.

Sometimes, the events that are incorporated into religion can compromise its purity. A religion without festivals is susceptible to becoming lifeless and boring for many people. Children and youths often find a religion they like through its religious festivals. They see the appeal of worship as its religious festivals.

Some people won't be content with just religious observances during a festival. They want to see some sort of outward, merry-making spectacle. To satisfy that need for faith-based satisfaction, ceremonies, rituals, processions, and festivals are created. While no one can deny that these practices are wrong, devotees must ensure that they are organized in a respectful manner.

Some holy days are only available to certain ethnic groups or Buddhist traditions. Two aspects are important to consider when considering Buddhist festivals.

With the exception of the Japanese, most Buddhists use the Lunar Calendar.

Dates for Buddhist festivals can vary from one Buddhist tradition to another and from one country to the next.

There are many Buddhist festivals. Some of the most important are:

Buddhist New Year

The new year in Theravadin, Thailand, Laos, Burma and Cambodia is observed for three consecutive days starting on the first full moon of April. The new year in Mahayana countries begins on the first full

Moon day of January. The Buddhist New Year is dependent on the country of origin and the ethnic environment of the person. According to the lunar calendar, Koreans, Chinese, and Vietnamese celebrate the New Year in February either late January or the end of January. The Tibetans celebrate usually one month later.

Vesak or Visakah Puja:

Vesak Puja (Buddha's Birthday Festivities) is the traditional name for Buddha's anniversary. This festival, which celebrates the birth, wisdom, and release of Buddha, is the most important festival for Buddhists. It's not held in leap years, but it is celebrated on the first full moon day in May. Vesak is the Indian name for the festival.

Loy Krathong

This Festival is held in Thailand at the end of Kathin Festival Season, when the rivers and canals are full of water. It takes place on the full moon night of the Twelfth Lunar Period. People bring pots of leaves, candles, and fragrance sticks to the festival and let them drift in the water. All bad luck is supposed disappear when these items are gone. Loy Krathong is a common practice that pays tribute to the sacred footprint of Buddha at the Narmada River in India.

The Plowing Festival

Two white oxen pull an oxen with a gold-painted plow when the moon is half-full in May. Four girls dressed in white scatter rice seeds from silver and gold baskets. This is to mark the Buddha's first moment in understanding. It was said to have happened when the Buddha, aged seven years old, left his ancestor to watch the plowing.

The Elephant Festival

Buddha used the example the wild elephant, which can be harnessed to make it easier to train. A person who is new to Buddhism should also have the friendship of an older Buddhist. Thais celebrate this saying with an elephant festival every third Saturday in November.

Festival of the Tooth

Kandy is a charming city in Sri Lanka. It's located on a small hill. A great temple was built to house the tooth of Buddha. Because the tooth is hidden in many caskets, it is not visible to us. There is however, a special procession that takes place once a year on August night, the night of full moon.

Avalokitesvara's birthday:

It celebrates the Bodhisattva ideal represented by Avalokitesvara who represents the perfect of compassion Mahayana traditions from China and Tibet. It takes place on a full moon day in March.

Chapter 14: Precept and Right Action

The body is an extension of the soul. We express ourselves through our actions

Our inner feelings and ourselves. All the different ways we use our bodies and emotions.

Our body is a mirror of our inner self. We leap in joy, then we bend in

Pain, don't be ashamed and do not give up.

Buddhism teaches that the mind and body do not exist as separate entities.

Extensions of one another. Intention and thinking influence the actions

It is also true that vice versa. Our actions have an impact on the environment.

How we think. Our minds will be forced to stand tall if we are unable to do so.

To think more highly of ourselves. It's not one-dimensional.

Everything is interconnected.

This book demonstrates the importance of taking action throughout the course of the book.

This has been mentioned numerous times. I've even gone so far as to state that action is everything.

Backbone of Buddhism Not philosophical debates or theological debates.

Questions are not for deity worship. What matters is the

Most important is our ability and willingness to take corrective action.

We discussed the importance of right view, intent and speech.

Change the way you live your life. Right action can have more positive effects

These are all more powerful than any of them taken together.

This is a good example of how it might look. You will find someone who is kind-hearted.

Very soft spoken. Because he is so friendly, people enjoy being in his company.

His kind words and encouraging nature inspire and motivate them. This is just the beginning.

The fact that this person is kind to his body and others.

Actions He helps others in need physically (he could even be a doctor).

He picks up the dead. His bodily actions are only a small representation of his.

Kind and generous heart. It would be great if it was so.

It would.

One common myth that I want to dispel is the notion of quite.

widespread. Right action doesn't include monetary spending. This is what it means.

The next section will discuss it. Right action does not refer to everything that

You can take care of your body by yourself, and that doesn't require external assistance.

Tools

Right action in Buddhism is defined as:

1. Abstinence is the best way to live.

2. You should not take what isn't yours.

3. Abstain from all sexual offenses

Abstinence is not a way to live a full and fulfilling life

The most vile thing anyone could do from his home is undoubtedly the most heinous.

To kill another human being would be an action. Even pack animals do

Not to kill other members of their pack. Sometimes humans do so.

They are addicted to lust, greed, and an inability to control their emotions.

Another life.

Buddhism doesn't dwell on the theological question about the origin

Nature of life. It does however teach its followers that the taking of

Life is not right because it causes suffering.

People often say that someone dies from something within them.

Commits murder. It is impossible to tell if it is true, but only a murderer can.

It makes sense theoretically. Every aspect of life has its consequences.

It is not different to take someone else's lives. It is easy to see it as a challenge.

It makes perfect sense to me that this would be true if you look at cause and effect from a point of view.

Take something from us to make someone else's life better.

Different schools of thought have different views on the existence of other beings.

Different opinions can be held. Some believe that all harm is bad

Life is dangerous and difficult. According to them, Buddha taught that life is dangerous and bad.

He meant abstinence from all forms of life and not just human life. It

It makes sense, because animal suffering can also be caused by eating. Eating

Meat is a luxury, but not a necessity. Modern

Science has also supported this conclusion. These schools of thought advocate for this.

vegetarianism.

Other rare schools of thought think that avoidance should be encouraged

It is not allowed to eat meat and take human life. But

It is best to avoid cruelty to animals and other living creatures.

It is against the spirit of Buddhism. To be cruel is to

Cruelty towards animals is unacceptable. There is no distinction.

You should not take what isn't yours.

Stealing is directly connected to a bad intention. Sometimes,

It is often a result of dire need, but it most likely has its roots in lust or undue.

desire. People would be able to control their desires and avoid the temptation of

Theft would cease to exist.

The act of stealing is often justified by the person who does it.

He/she believes that a small piece of bread, or one fruit from a tree, is enough.

It wouldn't really make a big difference. It is possible that the owner would not.

Even the thieves can see the difference. Sometimes, the thief even attempts to argue that

Because he could use the item (or steal it), stealing is actually his/her right.

Money) is more intelligent than its original owner.

These are all futile attempts at easing the conscience. I mentioned

We have said before that wrongdoing stirs the conscience. Stealing is another example.

It does exactly that. Instead of just listening, however,

Most people simply chose to calm down their emotions by telling lies.

Stealing can cause suffering for everyone. When a person begins to steal, it is a sign that they are serious about their cause.

Such a person can't stop on this path. One small theft can lead to another

The cycle continues until the catch, when everything is complete.

person him/herself suffers.

Abstinence from all sexual offenses

It is a method of procreation. It is also one the most primal means of reproduction.

pleasure. This is a human right.

Sometimes it can get out of control and cause damage to everyone involved

Get involved.

Buddhism, like Abrahamic religions does not view marriage as a problem.

It is a sacred matter. There aren't any clear guidelines about polygamy, or polyandry.

The rules of marriage. It only urges its followers to find a way.

This is a win-win situation for all and doesn't hurt anybody's feelings.

If you're in a committed relationship with defined boundaries, you should be careful

It is important to adhere to these boundaries and not move beyond them.

Most schools generally don't value promiscuity.

It is a source of chaos and destruction for society.

Consent is a key element that is clearly highlighted.

Without consent, there can't be rightful sexual intercourse.

Both the parties. Forcing someone to do something is only a recipe for suffering and pain.

sometimes even death.

Chapter 15: The Do's and Don'ts Of Buddhism

In the book, I mentioned the Eight Fold Path which was designed to help you get rid of all your suffering. The Eight Fold Path is a Buddhist path that will help you get rid of suffering and enjoy your life as much as possible. Let's look at the ways this can be integrated into our lives and clear up any preconceived notions you might have about Buddhism.

DO

These actions will help you make your life easier.

Right Sight

Keep in mind the truth and don't try to see things through a narrow lens. There are many perspectives. You can open yourself to greater understanding when you show empathy and don't judge the events in your life.

Do not see the world as biased. Take the world as it is. Instead of limiting your perspective, be more open to seeing the world as it is. This will allow you to have a better understanding and compassion for others.

Right Attitude

Be compassionate and show compassion in your daily life.

Do not think the world revolves around your actions and be selfish

Right speech

Think before you speak. Instead of being prejudiced against anyone, allow yourself to see the whole picture. Spread happiness by being kind and sincere with others.

Do not tell lies. Be kind to others. Unkind people always find their unkindness returning to them in the form karma or unhappiness.

Right Action

Do the right thing. Keep your eyes open and be present. Spread happiness and don't be afraid to show kindness to those who are in need.

Do not treat people in a disrespectful manner. Don't take actions that make other people unhappy. As a Buddhist follower, your responsibility is to spread happiness rather than to make other people unhappy.

Right Livelihood

Find the work you are passionate about. You can avoid the work that exploits other people if you're able. This is a sign that you are true to your profession. Believe in the work you do. If you don't believe in what you do, then you should look into your vocation.

Do not take advantage of others. To put others in a less advantageous position in your life to advance your own goals is not a winning trait.

Right effort

Don't be afraid to do the right thing. If you approach things with the right attitude you can make your efforts count.

Do not be lazy or apathetic. You may have periods in your life where you are less active than others, but it is not a sign of weakness or lack of effort.

Right Awareness

Remember that everyone in your world has a story to tell and that every decision you make can have an impact on the lives of others. Pay attention to your life and how you contribute to it. Mindfulness can help you be more aware of how you present yourself to others and your spiritual connection.

Do not think your opinion is the only one that matters. Each person is like a grain of sand. You can live your life in harmony with others if you're more aware of them. If you think that others don't matter, your life will be less fulfilling.

Right Meditation

Meditation can be incorporated into your daily life even if it means you need to wake up earlier. You will have a richer life. Understanding where you fit in the scheme of things will help you to live a more fulfilling life. Meditation allows you to be who you are and helps to understand your weaknesses and strengths. Meditation can help you get away from the worldly worries and problems life may throw at you. It allows you to use your intuition for solutions to any problems that arise along your path.

It's okay to not "get it", and that it may take you some time before you feel comfortable with meditation. You must train your brain to this discipline. After you practice it for a while, you'll be more awakened to the true meaning of Dharma.

Although the meaning of Dharma is well-known, in a limited sense it is about our protection from suffering and other problems. This is the purpose of the eightfold path. If you follow Buddhist teachings and live your life, you will find it easier to enjoy your life.

Siddhartha Gautama, who was born two centuries ago, came to his senses through the enlightenment he received. He is still with us today and will continue to be so as long as people learn about Buddhism and integrate any aspect of it into their lives. You will see why I wrote this book. I believe that Buddhism philosophy is a great way to live a happier life. It works. I know it works. The foundations of Buddhism are simple and simplify people's lives. This helps make life more worthwhile in these difficult times. That's what Siddhartha Gautama was trying to achieve when he embarked on his journey of discovery to discover why people suffer.

Chapter 16: What is Suffering?

"Attachment is the source of all suffering."
- Buddha

Perhaps it would be a good idea to first read the Parable of the Poisoned Arrow before we discuss the significance of suffering in Buddhism. It was actually the First Buddha who instructed it to Malunkyaputta.

It began when Malunkyaputta, a minister, was disturbed by reference to why Buddha remained silent on the Undeclared Question. These inquiries concern the existence of the world in time, space, individual personality, and life after death.

They look like the following:

Questions about the existence of the world in the present:

Is the world eternal?

Or not? ... Or both? Or both?

For inquiries about the presence of the universe in space:

Is there a limit to the size of the universe?

Or not? ... Or both? Or both?

For inquiries about individual characters:

Is the self defined differently from the body?

It is not unlike the body, however.

Inquiries on life after death:

Is the Buddha still alive after death?

Or not?

... Or both?

Or not?

He couldn't recognize the Buddha's silence to his questions so he moved forward to try to find the Buddha to answer these questions.

The Buddha informed him upon meeting him that he had never promised to clarify any definitive magical substances.

Malunkyaputta was then told the Parable of the Poisoned Arrow. This explained why such questions are not relevant to his lessons. This is the story: He would be offered to a specialist by his friends, confidants, and family, but he would insist that he wouldn't allow the bolt to be taken out until he could determine whether the man who shot him was an honorable warrior, a minister or a trader.

He would then say, "I won't have the bolt taken out until my discover the first name and last name of the man who shot... until until I find out whether he was tall or medium-sized... until he has brilliant, ruddy, or dim skin... until he discovers his home town, city or town...

Until I can determine if the bow used to shoot my was a crossbow, long bow, or a short bow; until I can tell if the bowstring that was used to shoot me is bark, ligaments, bamboo strings or fiber or hemp; until I can tell if the pole that was used to shoot me came from a wild or was it developed.

I will not know if the plumes that were attached to the pole to shoot me came from a stork or a peacock or a vulture until I find out if the pole used to shoot me was held together by the ligament of a water wild animal ox or bull or monkey.

The man would then say, "I won't have that bolt taken out until you see if it was a bended or typical bolt, an oleander, or spiked bolt."

He would then eat the dirt from the injury, but he could not know the truths behind these inquiries. Another reason the Buddha recommended this story was to expose man's inacceptability, or Dukkha. This is the root cause of all affliction. Let's now examine Dukkha.

The Three Categories of Dukkha Buddhist Lessons reveal the three types of Dukkha. The Dukkha-dukka, or the dukkha of painful encounters, is the first. This classification includes both mental and physical sufferings associated with the stages of birth, maturing, and death.

It refers to the pain and suffering that comes from doing something that does not bring joy. The Viparinama-dukka, or the dukkha that reveals the changing ways of all creatures, is the second. This classification is best described by the feeling of being confused or wanting more.

The third is the Sankharadukkha, or the dukkha with adapted understanding. This is the "essential inadmissibility" or the dukkha of adapted understanding. It is common in all types and types of existence since they all change, are never permanent, and have no inward substance or center.

It is a constant longing that can't be fulfilled. Many Buddhist teachings emphasize the importance of dukkha in everyday life.

It includes more than just the passage of time, such as death, illness, and maturing. It is as bad as being isolated from your closest friends.

Dukkha is the ability to not get what you need. A crucial Buddha concept concerning dukkha is the Five Clinging Aggregates. These are: Form (rupa), The type of any conscious being or protest is made up of the four components earth, water and fire (as described in the second chapter).

Sensation (vedana), also known as feeling or sensation, refers to an experience with the faculties of a person. It can be enjoyable, unpleasant, or impartial. Samnjna is the mental and tangible process of recognizing, names, and notifying. To see the feelings of joy and outrage, and the sizes and shades of the plants and animals, one can use observation.

Samskara - Mental Formations are all kinds of mental engravings or moldings that can be created by any protest. These also include any procedure that makes it possible to follow up on an item.

Cognizance (vijnana). This refers to being able to identify the parts and parts of any question. Diverse Buddhist lessons clarify

Consciousness as: Knowing something or having wisdom (as indicated in Nikayas/Agamas).

A collection of discrete, interconnected demonstrations of acumen which progress quickly (as indicated in the Abhidhamma). Some Mahayana writings indicate that all experience is established.

It is possible to find misery anywhere and everywhere. It can be found at any point where you feel connected to anyone, including your thoughts, words, actions, environment, friends, family, and body. It is best to follow the advice of Buddha and rehearse The Noble Eightfold Path to get rid of it.

You may have gained more insight into the Buddhist concept of Suffering and are now interested in learning more about Karma. This word is often used indiscreetly in the modern world by non-professionals. However, you will soon discover its true importance in the next part.

Chapter 17: Respecting your Posture

This may seem to have little to do with Buddhism. Meditation is about a particular stance. There are energy points in the body that are called chakras. This is why acupuncturists believe that balance is essential for good health. The Chakras are similar and run in a straight line, from the top of your head to the tailbone of an individual. Bad posture can cause problems with energy flow through your chakras. If you feel pains in your neck and shoulders when you're stressed, this could be because the chakra in your neck is blocked. Energy cannot pass through it. You need to understand the importance of posture and how it affects your response to life. Step 5 is about recognizing the importance of posture.

For meditation, the normal position is to sit on a yoga mat on a floor with your legs extended and your knees bent. Then, cross your ankles. There are more advanced positions, but they are not for beginners.

These positions are only for those who have mastered over years how to position their legs and feet in the full lotus position. This is impossible for most people. If you are unable to move, you can meditate on a hard seat. However, the most important thing is that your body remains centered. You can do this by placing your feet on a cushion or laying on your back. With your palms facing up, place your hands on one side of the cushion. Move your body around until it feels right. The ideal position is one that you are able to stay in during meditation without moving or tipping over. Your back will be straight, and this is a very important aspect of the right posture.

Posture in general

Your shoulders should not sag in everyday life. Crossing your legs can cause blood flow problems and restrict blood flow. When you're sitting in a chair, your feet should be flat on ground. While posture is often overlooked by many people, a monk meditating in a chair would have his back straightened. His hands will not be positioned one over the other. To support their weakest hand they place the strongest hand at the bottom. If you're right-handed, your right hand will be the strongest.

Because misalignment in the spine can lead to many ailments, posture is key. You can improve the way your body reacts to your lifestyle by eating mindfully. There are many exercises to help you respect your posture. You can join a local yoga class if you are interested. It's not trendy. You are more likely to find like-minded people taking yoga classes to improve mobility and life.

Yoga exercises can help increase mobility. However, they can also improve your breathing. This is crucial for yoga success. When you make movements, it is your breath that matters. A good yoga teacher can help you understand this.

The chakras are energy points that run from the top to the base of your spine.

One chakra is different because it is in the heart area. However, if you start to be gentle with people around you, this chakra will continue to allow energy flow. This is another reason to avoid anger.

Stretch regularly. Regular walks and standing straight when sitting can help mobility. You can also regain lost energy. You won't feel much better if you spend some time meditation instead of slouching in front of the TV. Remember that energy is what creates energy, even if you feel lethargic. Walking and engaging in the activities that are within your capabilities will help to open the chakras. Swimming is a great exercise that requires little impact and can improve your posture.

It is important to be aware of your posture. Bad habits can lead to a blockage of your energy centers, which will cause you to suffer. Siddhartha Gautama saw that many people were suffering from physical ailments. He developed his ideas keeping in mind that not all people are in top condition. He wanted to end suffering for all people, even the infirm. This chapter will help you improve your health and reduce your suffering.

Chapter 18: Buddha's philosophy - How does it integrate into your daily life?

Although you won't see immediate results from practicing Buddhism, it can help you to be patient and persevere. It is a religion that has helped millions to overcome their sufferings, and it has passed on its knowledge to others. Meditation is an important part of achieving enlightenment. This requires that the individual enters a Zen-like state where they seek the meaning of their lives. Their philosophy is to not cause harm to anyone. It requires effort, determination, discipline, and hard work. This modern life can also reflect the Buddhist philosophy. Are you a fan of yoga? Yoga can help you to feel calm and relaxed.

One of the many benefits of Buddhism is body regulation. Good mindfulness can help your brain regulate well. Even if you're stressed, your mind can still stay focused. You can get spiritual benefits as well as physical health from practicing

Buddhism. You will be able to behave in all situations. Mindfulness can improve your ability to live skillfully, rather than allowing yourself to be consumed by out-of-control worry and regret. Morality can also benefit from this. It's easy because Buddhism's philosophy places emphasis on moral values and conduct. This will allow you to pause before you make any actions that could cause pain or conflict.

The Five Precepts can also be used in daily life to prevent us from killing, stealing, having sexual misconduct, using drugs, and speaking rudely to other people. It is now part of our laws, which must be observed by all people. These philosophies were practiced many years ago, but people didn't know that Buddhism was a part of their current religion. Mindfulness can be helpful in managing anxiety disorders, including posttraumatic stress disorder. Evidence suggests that mindfulness meditation can help with anxiety disorders such as posttraumatic stress disorder. It encourages acceptance and not avoidance of negative emotions like sorrow.

Stories of Buddha in short can help us understand his philosophy. These are some of his most inspiring stories.

The Blind Men and the Elephant

One day there was a certain Raja who called his servant and asked him to go and gather all the Savatthi men who were born blind and show them an elephant. The raja said to the assembled blind men, "Here's an elephant." He presented each man the head, ears, trunk, back, tail, trunk and tail of the elephant. Each one believed that it was an elephant. After the men with blind eyes had touched the elephant, the Raja approached them all and asked, "Well, blind man. Have you ever seen the elephant?" They began to argue, "Yes it is!" "No, it is not!" They began to argue, "Yes it is!" and "No, that is not!" until they finally came to an agreement. The scene was a delight for "Brethren", the raja. "Just as these preachers, scholars, and others holding different views are blind and unseeing ....? They are ignorant of the fact that they are quarrelsome, disputatious and wrangling in their ignorance, but each still maintains reality as it is."

This story demonstrates how different people perceive the world. It also shows that everyone needs to have a deep understanding of one thing. People only believe in what they see. This story shows us how to see the world differently based on our own experiences, culture, languages, and cultures.

Another story is:

The Master and the Thief:

Shichiri Kojun, a Zen master, was reciting sutras one evening when a thief entered his home with a sharp blade demanding "Money, or life." Shichiri replied, "Don't disturb me!" You can get the money from that drawer. He resumed his recitation. This unexpected response shocked the thief, but he continued with his business. The master interrupted him as he helped himself to the money and said, "Don't take all of that." You can leave some money for me to pay tomorrow's taxes. The thief took some money with him and was ready to go. The master shouted at him just before he fled, "You took mine and didn't even than me!" It's not polite!" The master was shocked by the thief's fearlessness. The master thanked him and he ran off. Later, the thief told his friends that he'd never felt so scared in his entire life. The thief was captured and confessed to the theft of Shichiri's home a few days later. The master called him as a witness and he stated, "No, this guy did not steal anything from my house." I gave the money to him. He thanked me for it." He was so moved that he resolved to turn his back on me. After his release, the thief became a disciple and, many years later, achieved enlightenment.

This story shows us that we don't need to be burdened by any untoward events in our lives. It is important to let go of any pain that may make our lives difficult.

Remember that everything happens for reasons. Accept it and do good for others.

Buddhist Buddhism: The Most Important Lessons

Acceptance is one of the most important lessons Buddhism teaches. Acceptance is the first step to self-realization. Acceptance does not necessarily mean you should be sad, but it does mean accepting that yes, there is a way. It is true that you are sad. You are indeed sad. Realizing what you feel is one way to clear the space in your head without doing anything else that will destroy you. Buddhism is all about ending suffering and ending rebirth. Therefore, what the Buddha taught 2,500 year ago is still relevant today. Every day, practice the Eightfold Path.

Meditation and the Buddhist lessons can lead to enlightenment. Meditation is meant to raise pure awareness. Pure awareness is awareness that does not involve any thought. You should not stop thinking when it arises. The decision to stop thinking is itself a thought. Any type of hallucination should not be considered thought. Therefore, you should not pay attention to any visions or sounds that might arise. Anything you can feel, see, touch, or feel is an object, not the subject. Your eye cannot see what is happening around you, so the subject can't see it. Your brain and senses cannot perceive the "true" you that you seek. Meditation is best done in the morning, after a good night of sleep. Meditation should not be done when you are tired.

Although birth and death are a concept that continues individuality, it does not necessarily mean that the body will be transported to the next life. Neither will all the information stored in the brain pass on to the next life. This teaching is known as Law of Karma and is something we should seriously consider. It allows us to recognize and understand our fundamental nature. This will allow us to eliminate the uncontrollable and inevitable death and rebirth that is the source of all our suffering.

Truth of karma, empty spaces are often used to represent basic nature. This is to show its inability to discriminate and duality, as well as its unlimited time and space. Because the ultimate existence of a human being is this, the idea of birth or death is no longer applicable. It is not helpful to us to talk about basic nature because most of us are not enlightened. First, we need to understand the multi-life theory at its most basic level. This directly impacts our daily lives. Karma is an action or combination of actions by one being or group of beings that produces effects. The future of the person who performed the action will be determined by the effects. Good or bad karma has no effect on the future. It is simply a natural phenomenon that is controlled by natural laws. The round of cause-and-effect loses its meaning upon enlightenment. Samsara, also known as the round between birth and death, is over. Because basic nature transcends duality and is absolute, no one can receive any effect. You can practice it by helping the poor, being generous with others, offering prayers to the Buddha and saints of other religions, teaching others skills or knowledge that will help improve their lives, and you may even be able to reincarnate as a person with a bright future. All of the good qualities that make up our basic nature are found in it, including love, kindness, compassion and joy. These good qualities can lead to good karma which has positive effects. These good qualities can be discovered slowly as you cultivate harmony with the basic elements of nature. It's like a ray of sunlight breaking through heavy clouds. These revelations are the result of an individual's free will. This free will produces good karma and good karma leads to good effects, which in turn produce good karma for the next effect. A person can become enlightened and recognize their basic nature and become a Buddha.

The understanding and self-emptiness of oneself do not necessarily mean that you are done with life. It only means that you can begin living a happy, fulfilled life. It is a simple realization of an individual. But, in an enlightened state, it sees all people as if they were in a dream. It is impossible to attain enlightenment or identify with basic nature and become one with the universe without realizing that the idea of the self is not only dangerous but invalid. The self is defined in Buddhism as the desire for an unending existence or continuous life. The other component is attachment to one's own view. This is usually expressed as my view. Although attachment to one's own view is a gradual process over one's lifetime, it is influenced largely by one's past and karma. When views differ, and each entity claims the rightness or importance of their view, it can create a feeling of separation.

Source of Joy is only possible if you understand the root cause of your suffering. You can suffer from sickness or death. The five aggregates that make up the human experience, which is the body as well as the mind, are called suffering. These five aggregates include form, sensation and perception as well as conditioned function and consciousness. All human suffering stems from the human concept and attachment to body and mind. The realization of our fundamental nature is the only way to end suffering, just as with the concepts of birth and death and karma. Realizing your basic nature is essential to stop suffering. The body and mind appear to exist but are constantly changing and are not permanent. It's as if one could see oneself in a dream or as an actor playing a role. This is the realization of one's basic nature, which can be described as complete emptiness. It also means that there is no suffering.

Conclusion

As a Buddhist practitioner, I've seen many misconceptions about Buddhism around the world. This is why I am humbled to introduce you to Buddhism.

Try to incorporate the tips into your everyday life. It may seem daunting and difficult at first, but if you persevere, you will feel less stressed and happier.

Vipassana is a very useful and beneficial technique for beginners. This meditation technique can also be done at home. It's simple and not too complicated. You just need some peace and quiet, and time to yourself.

Best of luck with your journey!

www.ingramcontent.com/pod-product-compliance
Lightning Source LLC
Chambersburg PA
CBHW071832080526
44589CB00012B/992